Discipling
Generation Y

Published by
The Bible Reading Fellowship
15 The Chambers, Vineyard
Abingdon OX14 3FE
United Kingdom
Tel: +44 (0)1865 319700
Email: enquiries@brf.org.uk
Website: www.brf.org.uk
BRF is a Registered Charity

ISBN 978 1 84101 804 1

First published 2014

10 9 8 7 6 5 4 3 2 1 0

Acknowledgments
Unless otherwise indicated, scripture quotations are taken from The New Revised Standard
Version of the Bible, Anglicised edition, copyright © 1989, 1995 by the Division of Christian
Education of the National Council of the Churches of Christ in the United States of America,
and are used by permission. All rights reserved.

Scripture quotations taken from The Holy Bible, New International Version (Anglicised
edition), copyright © 1979, 1984, 2011 by Biblica (formerly International Bible Society), are
used by permission of Hodder & Stoughton Publishers, an Hachette UK company. All rights
reserved. 'NIV' is a registered trademark of Biblica (formerly International Bible Society). UK
trademark number 1448790.

Scripture quotations marked (GNB) are from the Good News Bible published by The Bible
Societies/HarperCollins Publishers, copyright © 1966, 1971, 1976, 1992 American Bible
Society.

Cover photo: Artens/Shutterstock.com

A catalogue record for this book is available from the British Library

Printed and bound by CPI Group (UK) Ltd, Croydon CR0 4YY

Discipling Generation Y

Themes from the book of Revelation

Steve Griffiths

This book is dedicated to the people who have inspired me and encouraged me throughout my faith journey so far. Particular thanks go to John Smith, for his wise and patient nurturing of my early faith; Dr George Bebawi, for giving me a love of systematic theology; Rev Dr Mike Thompson, for deepening my passion for the New Testament; and Professor Pete Ward, who has opened so many doors for me and encouraged me along the way.

As always, special thanks go to my wife, Jo, for her constant love and support.

Contents

Foreword 7

Introduction 9

1 Generation Y and the book of Revelation 13

2 Who is God? 26

3 What is the Church? 39

4 Who is Satan? 52

5 How do I understand suffering in the world? 65

6 What can I do about social injustice? 78

7 What is the final judgment of God? 91

8 What is salvation? 104

9 How important are worship and prayer? 116

10 How do I live as a disciple of Jesus? 127

Bibliography 140

Foreword

It was early in my career as Editor of *Youthwork* magazine when my friend, the author of this book, first leant across a dinner table and, with passion coursing through his veins, gave me both barrels about his pet peeve. Steve Griffiths, a man who had been committedly involved with young people since the earliest days of his ministry, was growing increasingly frustrated at the state of youth ministry publishing. While the shelves of the local Christian bookshop abounded with volumes of quick-fire ideas, ready-to-use meeting guides and discussion trigger resources (*mea culpa*), volumes of theological reflection on youth ministry were as rare as sightings of the Yeti.

Shifting subject somewhat, I must confess that I don't know too many people brave enough to write a book on John's Revelation. Strike that; I don't know an awfully large number of people prepared to preach a sermon on it. The final book of the Bible has always been a challenging read, filled as it is with strange imagery, prophetic messages and complex, multi-layered meaning. It has gained a reputation, rightly or wrongly, for being a 'difficult' book.

I am somewhat in awe of Steve, then, that he has managed to write an entire book about Revelation. Moreover, he's been able to publish a volume of theological reflection on youth ministry. Even more impressively, he has actually done the two things simultaneously, and that's what you hold in your hands: surely history's first ever book of reflections on Christian youth work as seen through the lens of the prophetic book of Revelation!

This book started life as a series of articles in *Youthwork* magazine. I have to confess that when Steve originally pitched the idea, I lacked the vision to see quite how it would work. When I read the first piece, however, my confusion was replaced by immediate appreciation. Steve had found a way to unpack and explore some of the big issues of youth discipleship—how we explore worship, spiritual warfare, and the role of the church with young people in the 21st century—through what seemed like the unlikeliest of mechanisms. By drawing these themes out from a book that is still largely unfamiliar book for most of us, he managed to find new insights, a new kind of relevance... and as a result our readers were hooked.

Those articles were a mere aperitif; you've just had the main course delivered to your table. This book uses the same principle but takes it much further; it drills deeper into both the book of Revelation and the vital question of how we disciple young adults. I am thrilled that Steve has written this book and, in so doing, contributed a valuable addition to the body of thinking and theology around ministry to the younger generations.

Martin Saunders, Director of Creative Development, Youthscape

Introduction

I gave my life to Jesus in 1984 at the age of 17. I will not take up your time by sharing my testimony, but suffice to say that it was a moment of real awakening, marking a huge shift in my lifestyle and behaviour. Having a naturally inquisitive mind, I immediately fell in love with theology. My life since that time has been marked by the quest for deeper knowledge and the sharing of my rather tentative findings with others, through writing, through preaching and through the training of youth work practitioners around the world.

Almost immediately after I became a Christian, certainly within a few weeks, I discovered the book of Revelation. Even though I struggled with the symbols and metaphors, it was as if a light had come on in my mind. I was entranced by this portion of scripture and dedicated myself to its study. As the years have gone by, I have become increasingly convinced that Revelation is the crowning glory of the Bible. Whereas Paul's letter to the Romans is unparalleled in taking us into the depths of the mystery of God's plan for salvation, John's letter to the seven churches in Revelation carries us to the pinnacle of the mountain, where we glimpse the cosmic glory of God's interaction with his created order. Revelation lays before us a vista barely comprehensible in its majesty, intensity and beauty. As far as I am concerned, Revelation makes sense of the rest of scripture. Everything that has gone before in the preceding 65 books of the Bible comes together in Revelation, in the context of both history and eternity. I am glad that it is the last book of the Bible. Nothing could possibly follow it.

My passion for theology has been equally matched by a desire to support youth workers in their ministry. Although I have been involved in a great deal of youth work through the years and have provided training for hundreds of youth ministry students and volunteers, I have never formally been a youth worker. I stand alongside those who are involved in this ministry. I am in awe of youth work volunteers and full-time youth workers because it is such a tough ministry, and that seems to be more the case today than ever before. Given what I have said above, I count it the deepest privilege of my professional life to share my thoughts on Revelation in this book with young people and those involved in discipling them.

Now for three disclaimers! First, this is not a commentary on the book of Revelation. While there is some very detailed exposition of certain passages, I am painfully aware of the gaps, which have been necessitated by the limited length of this book. Readers may be disappointed, for example, by my cursory treatment of the trumpets and the bowls of wrath, or they may feel frustrated by the lack of comment on the exact nature of the new Jerusalem. Revelation is such a complex and intensely detailed part of scripture that it would take a book three times the size of this one to begin to do justice to each theme. For those who encounter disappointment, I can only apologise, but I hope the insights offered on the passages that are explored in detail will more than compensate, and may even encourage you to undertake further research yourselves.

Second, this is not a book on the sociology of Generation Y. I am seeking to contextualise the book of Revelation within the activity of discipling young people. To that end, there is comment on Generation Y and some thoughts about the core values, identity formation and behavioural patterns inherent to this particular group of people. What I have to say in this regard derives both from the academic research of others and from my own observations and experiences, but those who are seeking a detailed sociological consideration of Generation Y will need to look elsewhere.

Third, my comments about Generation Y are inevitably generalisations. Any sociological framework that groups together millions of people will inevitably result in generalised observations. There will be ideas about Generation Y that run counter to your own experience. There will be other ideas that concur with your experience. The onus is on you to sift through the information, taking what is useful and discarding what is useless. However, I do believe that there is enough useful analysis of Generation Y for you to work with and to adapt for your own context.

Before moving to the text itself, I need to say a brief word about the delineation of the various generations. There has been much excellent research with regard to generational theory in recent years. Although there are slight differences of approach and variances as to the chronological dating of each generation, there is a fundamental agreement about the eras into which they were born. For the purposes of this book, I will be making mention of four specific generational groups, all of which are still active within the church at the time of writing. They are the Silent Generation (who, as children, were 'seen and not heard'), born between the 1920s and 1940s; the Baby Boomers (from the post-war 'baby boom'), born between the 1940s and 1960s; Generation X (a generation difficult to define, therefore the 'X-brand'), born between the 1960s and 1980s; and Generation Y, born between the 1980s and 2000s. I am aware that some generational theorists may want to query the exact dates mentioned here, but, as I have mentioned, this is not a book about generational theory so much as an exploration of how best to disciple Generation Y in the light of themes in the book of Revelation. For that reason, I sit lightly to any critique regarding generational delineations.

In order to be as useful as possible, this book is structured with ten short chapters, each one exploring a particular theme from within Revelation. I hope that this approach may prove useful for either personal learning or as material for a Bible study with young people and/or youth workers and volunteers. At the end of each chapter, I have included some questions to consider in the light of the preceding material, which aim to give food for thought.

Scripture quotations are taken from the NRSV unless otherwise indicated. Some Old Testament quotations are my own translation from the Septuagint (LXX), using Brenton's version (Hendrickson, 14th printing, 2011). Some quotations from the New Testament are also my own translation from the Greek, using the UBS version edited by Kurt Aland and others (United Bible Society, 3rd edition, 1983). These quotations are marked with an asterisk (*).

Finally, I conclude with a few words of thanks. I am profoundly grateful to my editor, Naomi Starkey, for encouraging me to write this book. Her wisdom in helping me gain structure and focus has been invaluable. It is always a pleasure to work with Naomi and BRF. I am also very grateful to Phoebe Thompson, Martin Saunders and Jamie Cutteridge for giving me space in *Youthwork* magazine to put forward my ideas in a series of short articles. I am indebted to the 'Word & Worship' congregation at St Mary's, Linton. Together we studied the book of Revelation over a nine-month period in 2012. Their feedback and interaction were very helpful as I honed my thinking on the application of this part of scripture. My deepest debt of thanks, as always, is to my wife Jo. She has been long-suffering and sacrificial in supporting me as I have worked on the material for this book. Only occasionally have her eyes glazed over as I have talked 'at' her about the implication of this or that Greek preposition, the breadth of Johannine vocabulary and potential interpretations arising out of this or that syntactical approach. I could not have written this book without her.

Chapter 1

Generation Y and the book of Revelation

Generation Y: the challenge of discipleship

When it comes to discipling young people, there has been an earthquake of epic proportions. The fault lines have ruptured, the landscape has been irrevocably changed and the old way of being in community together has gone for good. The map must be completely redrawn. This is deeply unsettling for those of us rooted in the values and behavioural patterns of previous generations. Trying to comprehend the worldview of Generation Y is, quite literally, akin to learning a new language. How can we possibly disciple a generation of young people who speak a different cultural language from the rest of us?

Despite the new language, though, the conversation remains the same. The purpose of discipleship is essentially what it always was. We are seeking to introduce young people into a way of living that takes seriously Jesus Christ as 'the way, the truth and the life' (John 14:6). We are mindful of Jesus' proclamation that 'I came that they may have life, and have it abundantly' (John 10:10). Ultimately, we want our young people to be happy and fulfilled, and our young people themselves want to be happy and fulfilled. As Christians, we believe that the only way to ultimate fulfilment is to live in a relationship with Jesus Christ. Doing what we can to facilitate and encourage that relationship is the process of discipling. However, when it comes to mentoring Generation Y, we make life much harder for ourselves by misinterpreting the end result of the process of discipling. It is crucial for us to get a thorough understanding of this before we move into a consideration of Revelation and the role it can play in the discipling process.

In Ephesians 5:1, Paul exhorts us to 'be imitators of God'. Furthermore, he tells us in Colossians 1:28 that his desire is to 'present everyone mature in Christ'. In our discipling of young people, we have traditionally developed a rather static model on the basis of such biblical ideas. That is to say, we have held to an idea of what Christ is 'like', in terms of characteristics, ethical values and behavioural patterns, and have trained our young people to exemplify this likeness in their own lives. In so doing, we have assumed that they are fulfilling Paul's command to 'imitate God'. Such an approach, however, is less likely to work for Generation Y, which understands personal authenticity much more in terms of flow and change than static adherence to a preconceived frame of being. To be effective in our discipling of Generation Y, we need a new perspective on the end result; we need to understand afresh what it means to be 'mature in Christ'.

We find help in the process of redefining discipleship from a rather unexpected source—Carl Jung. In 1932, he gave a paper at the Alsatian Pastoral Conference entitled 'Psychotherapists or the Clergy', in which he had this to say:

Are we to understand the 'imitation of Christ' in the sense that we should copy his life… or in the deeper sense that we are to live our own proper lives as truly as he lived his in all its implications? It is no easy matter to live a life that is modelled on Christ's, but it is unspeakably harder to live one's own life as truly as Christ lived his.

Jung's point is that Christ was the fullness of humanity because he learned to live his life in true authenticity. He was absolutely authentic to who he was as the Son of God. To 'imitate Christ' does not mean that we must attempt to 'replicate Christ' in our own beings but that we must pursue our own authenticity as children of God. In essence, God has made me to be me, and he has made you to be you. We only achieve what Paul calls 'maturity in Christ' when I am authentically me and you are authentically you. The process of discipleship is helping young people to discover their own authenticity in God, not an attempt to create what Martin Luther called 'little Christs'. Quite simply, 'What would Jesus do?' is the wrong question. The right question is, 'What would God have me do, *as me*, in this situation?'

This causes us to reassess our discipling methodologies with regard to Generation Y. If we need to frame the discipling process in terms of the pursuit of authenticity, we must create opportunities not only to teach but also to help them explore. Generation Y discipling must be an intensely creative activity. Catechesis may have a part to play but it can no longer form the whole, as it did with the Silent Generation and perhaps even the Baby Boomers. There are two key ideas that can help us in this.

The power of symbols

The first is that Generation Y is growing up in a semiotic environment, which is to say that symbols hold immense power for them. To a large extent, this is driven by the consumer culture of Generation Y. It really does matter if a young person wears Nike trainers or Adidas. It really does matter if they use a Blackberry or an iPhone. This is not because the products themselves are of particular importance but because there is a meaning inherent within the product that has symbolic power in youth cultures. Young people express who they are through the products they consume and the symbols they wear. We might even say that Generation Y resides in a semiotic world. As we disciple young people, we must be aware of the power and meaning that reside in the symbols they use. We must be careful to interact with their symbols with deep respect, knowing that if we disrespect the symbols, we disrespect them.

15

With regard to our current study, it is deeply encouraging that young people understand the power of symbols and are content to express themselves in symbolic ways, because the book of Revelation is utterly reliant on symbolic language to express its teaching. Many people fear the book of Revelation because they take the contents as literal. They believe that all the events will take place as described by John. However, understanding these events as literal goes against the grain of scripture. Revelation is part of a writing genre known as 'apocalyptic', which uses symbolic language to describe spiritual realities that are too deep and profound for description. There is a great deal of apocalyptic genre in the Bible (for example, Ezekiel, parts of Daniel, parts of Isaiah, Mark 13 and sections of Paul's letters to the Thessalonians) and it was a widespread tradition of writing in Judaism and in other Middle Eastern religions. We shall see that many of the symbols in Revelation are used in other apocalyptic writings, which makes interpretation all the easier for us. By contextualising Revelation within the apocalyptic tradition, we are encouraged to understand its teachings as 'true' but not 'literal'. That is to say, the 'events' of Revelation will happen but not necessarily in the way that John describes them, because he is working within the limitation of human language to describe spiritual 'truths' that, by definition, are indescribable. Like Generation Y, John was content to create a semiotic world; he used symbols to speak of truths too deep for ordinary language.

The symbolic nature of John's vision is apparent to us from the very beginning of Revelation. In 1:10, he writes, 'I heard behind me a loud voice like a trumpet' (NIV). The Greek word used here for 'loud' is *megalein* (like 'megaphone'). However, this word does not refer to volume so much as grandeur: John heard a 'grand' voice like a trumpet. In those days, as in ours, trumpets were used when royalty was about to enter the room, and that is what is about to happen here: John is saying his prayers and a grand voice, like a trumpet, announces to him that something special is about to happen. Royalty is about to appear: John is about to be given a vision from the King of kings and Lord of lords.

John continues in verse 12, 'I turned round to see the voice that was speaking to me' (NIV). This is a strange phrase because we cannot see a voice; we can only hear it. But the word John uses for 'see', *blepein*, can have more to do with understanding than physical sight. The equivalent in English may be when someone explains a problem that you have struggled to understand and you say, 'Oh, I see!' So when he says, 'I turned round to see the voice', John means that he gave the voice full attention in order to understand the message. His use of the word *blepein* contrasts with the next part of this verse, where he says, 'And when I turned, I saw seven lampstands.' The word for 'saw' used here is different: it is *eidon*. Although not exclusively, this word often carries an even deeper meaning of sense perception. The English equivalent might be, 'I saw the wind blowing' or 'I saw fear in her eyes.'

It seems, therefore, that John did not *see* the vision he records in a literal and physical sense. Rather, it was a matter of spiritual perception in his mind's eye, as the Holy Spirit inspired him to 'see'. The understanding of this style of writing should take something of the fear out of our study of Revelation. The events described are not so much actual 'events' to happen but spiritual 'realities' described in symbolic language. As we move through our study together, we shall see that all the key themes of the Christian faith are revealed to John, and to us, so that we can gain assurance and comfort from God in our times of struggle and anxiety. It is incumbent on us, then, to teach Revelation to young people in such a way that God's original intent is honoured and their faith is deepened accordingly. The fact that Generation Y readily accepts symbolism as a method of transmitting truth should be a real encouragement to us.

Finding our authentic identity

The second helpful key idea is that young people are on a passionate quest to find their identity. The truth is that young people today are dissatisfied with the world, and, as a result, many are dissatisfied with life. Even if they do not vocalise it as such, young people are on a spiritual search. They are growing increasingly distrustful of the machinery of society as the provider of meaning and increasingly reliant on their friendship groups, whether physical or virtual, to discover identity and purpose. Paradoxically, the search for meaning, the spiritual quest, is becoming more and more individualised, yet it is still thoroughly worked out in community. As we shall see in a later chapter, the notion of 'belonging' is a core value for Generation Y. It is by 'belonging' that many young people discover their authentic identity.

Those of us who are observers of Generation Y often interpret their approach to life as deeply fragmented. From the outside, it seems that young people today labour under the weight of many 'identities'—one within the home, one at college, one at church, one or more online, one with the extended family and so on. Some young people are forced into this situation, particularly those from ethnic backgrounds who struggle to work out what it means to be, for example, a British Asian. Even for those young people who do not have these pressures, however, the creation of different personas according to context is an habitual way of being. Furthermore, they do not recognise this as fragmentation at all. Rather, their understanding of 'self' is not as one static unit but the sum total of what we might recognise as 'multiple identities'.

Rather than creating a problem, this can have profoundly positive implications for our discipling of young people. Through Revelation, we become convinced that authentic identity is, as Generation Y has discovered, a matter of multiplicity rather than one static concept. This is not least because of our dual location: we reside in two quite different places. John writes in 1:9 that he is 'in Christ' but also that he is 'on Patmos'. He recognises that he has a spiritual location (in Christ) and a physical location (on Patmos). He reiterates this dual location in verse 10 by stating, 'On the Lord's Day I was in the Spirit' (NIV). Again, we see two separate locations, one of physicality (on the Lord's Day) and one of spirituality (in the Spirit). So John gives us two locations for existence through four phrases—'in Christ/in the Spirit' (spiritual) and 'on Patmos/on the Lord's Day' (physical). He recognises a dual identity: we are citizens of heaven but also citizens of earth.

It would be true to say that many of the difficulties young Christians face are primarily a result of working out the tensions felt between their heavenly location and their earthly location. The temptations they face, the sins they fall into, are a result of the fact that they know Christians should behave in one way (spiritual location), but the pull of the body is too great to resist (earthly location). Engagement with Revelation can help them to understand that tension better and, crucially, learn to live with it in a positive sense. Through Revelation, we learn that the task of life is not to dissolve our multiple identities but to resolve them all into Christ. In verse 9, John refers to 'the suffering and kingdom and patient endurance that are ours *in* Jesus' (NIV). We are *in* Jesus—united with him—through suffering and glory, through joy and pain. Paul writes about this idea in Romans 6:3–5: 'All of us were baptised *into* Christ Jesus… If we have been united with him like this in his death, we will certainly also be united with him in his resurrection'*. We are integrally linked to Jesus: we are in him through the experience of suffering and glory that we share. In Christ, our multiple identities are resolved into a coherent sense of self, which is our authentic being.

The task of discipling Generation Y inevitably involves helping them to resolve their identities into Christ. This may take an enormous shift of consciousness for those of us who have not thought in these terms before. Those of us with a different world-view from Generation Y's may perceive the notion of multiple identities as confusing, chaotic, even spiritually schizophrenic. Our natural impulse is to encourage the young people to dissolve what we see as the disparities in their existence. While that may be an honourable pastoral intent, we must accept the fact that it is little more than the imposition of our worldview on to theirs. It is certainly nothing less than spiritual and pastoral colonialism.

Revelation and the discipling of Generation Y

Winston Churchill once described the Soviet Union as 'a riddle wrapped in a mystery inside an enigma'. That is a good description of how many of us view the book of Revelation! It is the portion of scripture that is least understood and causes the most amount of fear. As a result of that fear, many Christians decide to ignore it completely, which is a shame because it contains deep encouragements for us and can be a very useful tool in discipling young people. Most, if not all, of the key themes of faith are explored in Revelation, and so a systematic and creative approach will engage young people with the full gospel.

We must also acknowledge the fact that a great deal of erroneous teaching on Revelation has been given in recent years. In an attempt to 'tickle the ears of their hearers' (2 Timothy 4:3*), some popular authors have tended towards sensationalist approaches, inappropriately focusing exposition on certain passages in a noncontextual fashion. Whatever else we may say about Generation Y, they are generally hungry for truth. It is a sad fact that many young people gain all their knowledge about Revelation from these sensationalist readings. It is unhelpful to the process of Generation Y discipleship to fill their heads with non-contextual ideas about the rapture, Satan, the number of the beast, the identity of the 144,000, details about the second coming, the final judgment and so on. Therefore, we have a duty to teach Revelation responsibly to young people so that they are not unduly influenced or frightened by irresponsible authors.

Most theologians believe Revelation to have been written by the disciple John, who was with Jesus throughout his ministry. The only disciple not to be martyred for the faith, he became bishop of Ephesus and lived into old age. We know from Revelation 1:9

that John was on the island of Patmos 'because of the word of God and the testimony of Jesus' (NIV). This suggests that he had been sent into exile because of his ministry. Since Revelation was composed about AD96, he would have been about 80 years old at the time. Christians were living under the rule of the Roman Emperor Titus Flavius Domitian, who demanded veneration from all people within the Roman Empire, taking the title 'Lord and God'. Consequences were dire for those who refused to submit to him. That is not to say, however, that Christians were suffering terrible persecution. There was no bloodbath, with Christian martyrs being slain for holding fast to the gospel, under Domitian. It was not until the third century, under Emperor Diocletian, that persecution of Christians reached its height. Nevertheless, they were very difficult days to stand up for the faith and, crucially, refuse to venerate the Emperor. Christians suffered greatly as a result, primarily through economic and social marginalisation as well as being victims of slander, misunderstanding and abuse.

John's Revelation was sent to seven churches within his area of episcopal oversight—Ephesus, Smyrna, Pergamum, Thyatira, Sardis, Philadelphia and Laodicea. A messenger took his letter to these churches, journeying for more than 200 kilometres on a circular route, the main road in Asia Minor (modern-day Turkey). The churches where he stopped varied in size, power, wealth, faithfulness, doctrinal purity, style of worship, passion and the pursuit of God. To each church was delivered a highly personalised message, yet, taken together, these messages speak as powerfully to us today as they did to the first hearers. As we have already noted, symbolic language is at the heart of Revelation. That is not least the case regarding the use of numbers, and the most common of these used by John is 'seven', a biblical number for wholeness and completeness. Therefore these letters are written to seven separate, historical churches but they are also meant for every church—the whole Church—throughout time.

In 1:1, we are told that the book is 'the revelation of Jesus

Christ'. The word 'of' is crucial because of its ambiguity. It could mean the revelation 'about' Jesus Christ or it could mean the revelation 'which Jesus Christ gave to John'. The rest of the verse helps us understand better: 'The revelation of Jesus Christ, which God gave him [Jesus] to show his servants what must soon take place; he made it known by sending his angel to his servant John.' There is a hierarchy of revelation here. It is God's revelation; God gives it to Jesus; Jesus gives it to an angel; the angel gives it to John; John gives it to the Christians.

Furthermore, we must not overlook the importance of the phrase 'what must soon take place'. Many people take the book of Revelation to be speaking about things that will happen only at the time of the second coming, but John is clear that, for these Christians in AD96, the events would *soon* take place. We will see that there is a lot of reference in Revelation to the final days before the second coming but we must avoid what is called a 'futurist reading', realising instead that the teaching in this book is relevant to us in the here and now, not just some time in the future. Avoiding a futurist reading is best achieved by understanding the structure of the book of Revelation as cyclical, not linear. That is to say, Revelation reflects on the same period of history from different perspectives. The period of history considered is the time between the first coming of Christ and the second coming and it is explored from seven separate perspectives. We should not be surprised that there are seven perspectives, given that the number seven indicates 'completeness': this is a complete picture of the history of the world in that period. Each time that period of history is considered, there is something new to see, with the seven viewpoints each giving a new perspective, a different and fresh take on reality.

The seven cycles are as follows:

- Revelation 1:1—3:22: Jesus Christ and the seven churches
- Revelation 4:1—7:17: A view of the world from heaven
- Revelation 8:1—11:19: The warnings from God in history

- Revelation 12:1—14:20: Spiritual warfare in the world
- Revelation 15:1—16:21: Final judgment and its impact
- Revelation 17:1—19:21: God's judgment on civilisation
- Revelation 20:1—22:21: The destruction of Satan and the new world order

Revelation therefore proves useful as a tool for discipling Generation Y because it presents a complete narrative by which we can understand the flow of history. This is perhaps more crucial today than ever before. Generation Y is growing up in an uncertain world. There are wars and rumours of wars, there is economic turmoil on an unprecedented scale, and civil disorder and the threat of terrorism have become everyday experiences. The prospect of long-term unemployment and economic marginalisation is very real. Concerns over access to affordable education determine life choices at an early age. In all this, Generation Y is learning to live with a heightened level of anxiety that was not present for the preceding Generation X or Baby Boomers. While we acknowledge that there have been previous moments of heightened anxiety (for example, the Cuban missile crisis, the Vietnam war, the collapse of Communism, mass unemployment in the 1980s and '90s and so on), they have not been sustained to the level that Generation Y is currently experiencing.

The book of Revelation speaks deeply into that experience of heightened and sustained anxiety. Essentially, it is a prophecy given by God to struggling Christians, giving hope and encouragement in the face of their trials. It is a message of love, freedom and forgiveness, offering identity and dignity as citizens of the kingdom of God and leading us into our destiny as a royal priesthood. It confirms that God has been active throughout history and it assures us that God is in control of future events too. It confirms that God is sufficient, almighty and all-powerful and in him is contained all wisdom and knowledge, might and authority. This is exactly the experience of God that Generation Y needs at the present time. No matter how discouraged they may feel, no matter how hard it may be to understand the twists and turns of life, young people must be convinced that they are not alone. The Messiah walks alongside them in their anxiety and fear for the future. Crucially, there is purpose for their lives.

That message of encouragement and solidarity in anxiety is the heartbeat of Revelation. In 1:9, John introduces himself as 'your brother and companion in the suffering and kingdom' (NIV). This is an intensely pastoral approach, given the situation his readers were in. John could have pulled rank on them but chose not to. By right, he could have said something like, 'From Bishop John...' or 'From John, an apostle of Jesus Christ...' or 'From John, the disciple Jesus loved...' but he does not do that. Instead, he stands alongside them in their suffering: 'John, your brother and companion in the suffering and kingdom'. John knew that Christians are bonded together in love, so he reiterated the equality we share, regardless of professional calling. There is no hierarchy in the kingdom. We are all brothers and sisters together, equal in the eyes of God, regardless of age or maturity of faith. Elsewhere, Paul had said to Timothy, 'Let no one despise your youth' (1 Timothy 4:12). John exemplifies this approach by drawing alongside his hearers as a fellow sufferer and companion. We are therefore encouraged to draw alongside young people in their reading of Revelation with humility and a sense of equality. As we do so, we shall learn together the truths of the Christian gospel and be drawn deeper into the ultimate reality, which is God. It is the nature and being of God that is the subject of our next chapter.

Some questions to consider

- What has been your previous experience of the book of Revelation? If you had to choose three words to describe how you feel about this part of scripture, what would they be?
- What is the experience of the book of Revelation among the young people you work with?

- How do you feel about the idea that this part of scripture is not 'literally true' but contains 'spiritual truths'? How does that accord with the way you have understood the Bible in the past?
- What symbols are important to the young people you work with? How do they use those symbols? What meanings are inherent within them?
- In what ways do your Christian young people struggle with their 'dual location', being citizens of heaven while living here on earth?
- Where do the young people you work with form their multiple identities? How do you see them holding these identities in tension?
- What are the anxieties you recognise as being prevalent for Generation Y? What do you want young people to know of God to help them through these anxieties?
- What does it look like when a young person learns to resolve their identities into Christ? What does it mean for them to find themselves 'in Christ'?

Chapter 2

Who is God?

Generation Y: perceptions about God

Let's be honest. Generation Y does not care about God.

Well, that might be a slight exaggeration, but there is an underlying truth to the statement. We do not need to spend time reviewing the figures of decline in church attendance, because it would be too depressing, but we do know that a generation of young people is here today that does not have God on its radar. This is hardly surprising. Their grandparents, the Baby Boomers, began to sit more lightly to church attendance from the 1960s onwards. Their parents, Generation X, dragged along to church for Christmas and Easter and the occasional school assembly, may have had some contact with the local church youth club, but the pursuit of God was not high on their agendas once they found work and got married. So Generation Y is 'third generation unchurched'. There is no compulsion from the family for them to attend church and, in an increasingly social media-saturated environment, there is little sense that the local church can provide anything useful that the screen cannot. This is not to say that Generation Y is unspiritual. Nothing could be further from the truth, and we will have more to say about this in Chapter 4. However, spirituality does not necessarily equate to a belief in God, still less any identification with the God of Christianity.

When it comes to mission to Generation Y and the ongoing process of discipling, this lack of identification is not necessarily a bad thing. Previous generations of disciples have often had to 'unlearn' negative images about God in order to encounter the God of love revealed in Jesus Christ, but young people in Generation Y often have no image of God to begin with, so they have nothing to unlearn. They may have little comprehension of the Christian narrative, or none at all. As I write this, it is three weeks before Christmas. Two nights ago, I was sitting with a group of young people who hang around in the graveyard outside our church. I had bought some Chinese takeaway and we were sitting together in the cold, munching on pork balls and barbecued spare ribs and chatting about various things. Then we got on to talking about the Christmas story, and one of them said to me, 'Where does this Mary live, then?' He had absolutely no idea about the birth of Jesus in Bethlehem 2000 years ago. Although that may seem shocking to those of us of an older generation, we should not be disheartened. Often, the result of having no preconceptions concerning the Christian story is that young people have an attitude of enquiry and receptivity that is a fruitful seedbed for growth in discipleship.

If we want to disciple Generation Y believers, we must think very carefully about the image of God that we teach them. In each generation, there is a predominant image of God that is appropriate to their social context. We must be prepared to 'image' God in a way that is appropriate for the current generation of young people.

At the heart of this generational approach to God is a nuanced understanding of 'authority'. The Silent Generation respect authority because it is attached to a title or position in society—so the squire is respected, as is the vicar, the policeman and the bank manager. The Baby Boomers respect authority when it has been earned, so a self-made millionaire businessman is respected and a charismatic church minister with a large congregation is respected, alongside others who can show evidence of success and power in their sphere of work. Generation X is generally suspicious of authority figures, with a deeper concern to exercise personal authority. Generation Y have a far more questioning approach to authority. This approach is not necessarily negative, far less aggressive. Rather, Generation Y are very willing to respect authority figures but will pre-empt any acceptance with the question 'Why?'

These generational differences inevitably have an impact on the understanding of God as Father, the ultimate figure of respect. The Silent Generation tend towards living in obedience and fear of this authoritative deity. Baby Boomers regard the Father as the ultimate 'success story' and respond in praise and worship to the one who brings healing and forgiveness. Generation X will worship a God who allows freedom of expression and creativity in discipleship. Generation Y want to explore the depths of God as Father with a healthy, questioning spirit before committing themselves in discipleship.

At the heart of each generational disposition is the idea of relationship between the believer and God. Each generation understands itself to be 'in relationship' with God. The question is, how is that relationship to be lived out?

God as Trinity

At the heart of the Christian faith is our belief in God as Trinity—three Persons but one God. We make a fundamental error in our discipling of young people if we try to explain the Trinity as a doctrine to be understood. There is no way we can ever understand such a deep truth: the nature of God is beyond all comprehension. The more we try to 'explain' the Trinity, the more confused young people get, and this often proves to be a barrier to faith. In discipling Generation Y, we must learn a different approach. Rather than trying to get young people to 'understand' God as Trinity, we must help them to 'experience' God as Trinity. It is when the Trinity becomes an experience of the heart rather than a doctrine for the head that young people mature as disciples.

It is perhaps not surprising that John does not give any doctrinal teaching on God as Trinity in Revelation. It would be many years yet before the church was able to vocalise a belief in a trinitarian God. In AD96, there had been no clear statement or formulation of a belief in God as Father, Son and Holy Spirit. That is not to say, however, that John has nothing to say about God as Trinity. Indeed, he describes our experience of God in trinitarian terms from the very beginning of his letter, in 1:4–5, where he greets the seven churches thus: 'Grace to you and peace from him who is and who was and who is to come, and from the seven spirits who are before his throne, and from Jesus Christ, the faithful witness, the firstborn of the dead, and the ruler of the kings of earth.'

First, we note that grace and peace come from him 'who is and who was and who is to come'. This is a reference to God the Father that draws our minds back to Moses on Mount Sinai in Exodus 3. There, Moses was speaking with God and said, 'If I come to the Israelites and say to them, "The God of your ancestors has sent me to you", and they ask me, "What is his name?" what shall I say to them?' God said to Moses, "I am who I am"' (vv. 13–14). This is the name that God gives for himself—'I am who I am'—but there are no tenses in it, so we could also render it, 'I was who I was' or 'I will be who I will be.' All three are correct. When John defines God as 'him who is and who was and who is to come', he is pointing back to God's self-definition and confirming to his first readers that the God of Revelation is the same God who has been worshipped for hundreds of years.

The next phrase in verse 4 is, 'the seven spirits who are before his throne'. This is an interesting description of the Holy Spirit. As noted in the previous chapter of this book, the number 'seven' is very important in Revelation (there are more than 50 references to it) and it is a biblical number meaning completeness, totality and wholeness. As John writes to the seven churches, which represent the whole Church throughout time, it is natural for him to refer to the Holy Spirit as the 'seven spirits' in order to indicate the truth that the Holy Spirit dwells in each and every church in equal measure. There is only one Holy Spirit, of course, but he is equal and wholly present in every church throughout time. Hence he is described here as the seven spirits, a symbol of completeness and fullness.

Verse 5 gives us a threefold reference to Jesus Christ. First, he is described as 'the faithful witness'. The Greek word that John uses here is *martus* ('martyr'). However, this is not a reference to the death of Christ so much as the fact that he was faithful in bearing witness to the love of God throughout his life. Second, he is the 'firstborn of the dead'. This is a reference to his own resurrection and implies that we too will know resurrection. Third, he is the 'ruler of the kings of the earth'. This description of the Messiah is an allusion to Psalm 2:7–11, which says:

I will tell of the decree of the Lord: he said to me, 'You are my son; today I have begotten you. Ask of me, and I will make the nations your heritage, and the ends of the earth your possession. You shall break them with a rod of iron, and dash them in pieces like a potter's vessel.' Now therefore, O kings, be wise; be warned, O rulers of the earth. Serve the Lord with fear.'

John gives this title to Jesus because the early Christians were facing troubled times at the hands of Domitian and needed to be reminded that the Roman Empire was not the ultimate power. Domitian may have liked the title 'Lord and God' but Jesus Christ is the ruler of the kings of the earth—a message of comfort that the Christians desperately needed to hear.

In these two verses, then, we have an incredible description of God as Trinity. However, this description is not so much doctrinal as experiential. He is the eternal Father, who transcends time and space to be in relationship with us. He is the Holy Spirit, dwelling in completeness and fullness throughout his whole Church. He is the Son, the Messiah long ago prophesied who bears witness to the grace and peace of God, our guarantee of resurrection and eternal life, ruler over all.

Leading young people into an experience of the Trinity is at the heart of successful discipleship. Unlike previous generations, which grappled to understand the doctrine, Generation Y believers have a natural disposition towards the experience of Trinity. That is because they see relationships as fluid, dynamic and constantly changing. Many youth workers refer to this idea as 'flow'. Young people surf their way through a network of relationships in the same way that they surf the internet; interactions rise and fall in terms of intimacy and longevity in a manner that those of us of an older generation find difficult to comprehend. Facebook has transformed the meaning of the word 'friend'. For Generation Y, social networking has transformed relational interaction such that it is now akin to a barn dance: friends link arms, spin around and laugh together before moving on to the next partner with no sense of rejection or loss. After all, there is a whole room full of people to meet and laugh with. Relationship has become 'flow'.

This is little different from the doctrine of the Trinity as outlined by the Cappadocian Fathers in the fifth century. They taught the idea of Trinity as *perichoresis*, which images the Father, Son and Holy Spirit in an eternal dance together. Salvation occurs when we are invited into the dance. So Generation Y are happy to encounter a trinitarian God—the God of the dance, the God of flow, the fluid God who invites them into a relational mode of being that is constant only in its changeability and movement.

God the Father

Just as the Trinity is described in experiential terms, so we would expect the same to be true of the description John gives of God as Father. Of course, the very term 'Father' implies the experience of relationship, and John outlines the nature of our relationship to God the Father by exploring his characteristics. This is most especially true in his description of the Father in Revelation 4. Here, John does not offer a description of what the Father looks like; that would be impossible to do. Instead, he describes the characteristics of the Father by way of metaphor, in terms of colours and jewels.

He begins in verse 3 by stating, 'And the one who sat [on the throne] had the appearance of jasper and carnelian.'* Jasper is a clear, translucent jewel, so John is referring to the purity that emanates from the throne of God. Carnelian, as a red stone, symbolised anger and divine judgment. Interestingly, in Exodus 39:8–21, there is a description of the breastplate worn by the high priest, on which there were four rows of jewels, twelve in all, to represent the twelve tribes of Israel, the people of God. The first jewel listed is carnelian and the last is jasper, so perhaps John is reminding us that, just as the high priest held the people of Israel close to his heart, so God holds us close to his heart in heaven.

In the second part of Revelation 4:3, we are reminded of the culmination of the flood story (Genesis 9:16), as we read, 'A rainbow that shone like an emerald encircled the throne' (NIV). The fact that it encircles the throne, rather than being just an arc above it, symbolises the all-embracing totality of the Father's mercy and grace. Emphasising the breadth of the Father's love, this jewel is described as being 'like an emerald' but, in the original Greek, it is a translucent jewel that refracts the rainbow and spreads its colours out on to everything else. God's mercy and grace spread out over his whole creation.

In verse 6, John states, 'Also in front of the throne there was what looked like a sea of glass, clear as crystal' (NIV). There are two things to note here. First, the sea is often used in scripture as a metaphor for chaos and disorder. That is why the stories of Jesus calming the storm and walking on the water are so important, because they speak of Jesus bringing order out of chaos. In Revelation 21:1, we read that there is no sea in the new Jerusalem, meaning that there is no chaos or disorder in heaven. Second, in 4:6 the sea is like glass. It is pure and signals a distance between God and creation. The sea of glass reminds us that God is unique, holy and set apart.

Commentators generally agree that Generation Y desires transparency and purity, relationality and understanding from its authority figures. Young people are not averse to showing respect to those in authority, but will do so only if that respect is founded on the integrity of the leader. The picture that John paints of the Father embraces the characteristics that so many young people look for in their authority figures today—purity, grace, compassion and relationality. If he is introduced to young people as such, we may find that they are willing to enter a relationship with their heavenly Father.

It is a deep sadness to me that, in recent years, some within the church have tried to 'explain away' the idea of God as Father. I am sensitive to the need for gender awareness and to the fact that many young people have not had a positive experience of a father figure in their lives. However, neither of these is a good reason for us to abandon the idea of God as Father in favour of a more gender-neutral concept. In Revelation, John gives us a picture of God as Father that is intensely positive. The fatherhood of God encompasses what we might think of as feminine characteristics— mercy, grace, compassion, forgiveness—as well as those that we might see as masculine characteristics, such as judgment, wrath and anger. As we shall see, however, even the more masculine characteristics are set in the context of the feminine. God's wrath, for example, is set in the context of his compassion for the martyrs who have been slain, and God's judgment on sin is set in the context of his mercy towards sinners. I am reminded of Rembrandt's painting, *The Return of the Prodigal Son*. If we look closely at the hands of the father embracing his son, we see that one hand is that of a man and the other is that of a woman. Such is the embrace of God the Father to us.

Generation Y is smart. Young people today understand the complexity of relationship and the complexity of emotional responses. We do not need to be apologetic about portraying God as Father. Generation Y gets it.

God the Son

There is, of course, much teaching about God the Son in Revelation. The person of Jesus Christ infuses and informs the whole book. However, in the first chapter, John gives a vivid description of the appearance of the Son of Man, using picture language to illustrate the personality and nature of Jesus Christ.

He begins in verse 13 by stating that Jesus is 'dressed in a robe' (NIV). In the culture of the day, a long robe acted as a symbol of authority. It may also be a reference to the priestly role of Jesus, our high priest, drawing our minds to Exodus 28:4 in which the priesthood of Aaron is denoted, in part, by his beautiful robe. In Revelation, we are told that the robe was 'reaching down to his feet and with a gold sash round his chest'. The sash, a tight belt, is a reference to the ascension of Jesus. Workmen wore their belts around their waists, but Jesus' belt is pulled up to his chest. He is a workman no more: his work is complete and he has ascended to glory. The fact that it is gold strengthens this interpretation because that was the inheritance of royalty and a symbol of great wealth.

In verse 14, John notes that 'his head and his hair were white as white wool'. Daniel 7:9 gives a description of the Ancient of Days, the Judge of the world, which includes the words, 'the hair of his head was white like wool' (NIV). So here in Revelation we have a reference to Jesus Christ as Judge of the world. Moreover, John says, 'His eyes were like blazing fire' (NIV)—and in Daniel 10:5–6, the Judge of the world is described thus: 'Before me was a man dressed in linen, with a belt of the finest gold… His face was like lightning, his eyes like flaming torches.'* When Christ stands in judgment over the world, his eyes will pierce into us and nothing will remain hidden from him. Consolidating this idea, John moves on in Revelation 1:15 to say, 'His feet were like bronze glowing in a furnace' (NIV). Again this accords with Daniel 10:6, where we read, 'His arms and legs [were] like the gleam of burnished bronze' (NIV).

Verse 15 also attests to the divinity of Christ in the words 'and his voice was like the sound of rushing waters' (NIV), as this is the description of God in Ezekiel 43:2: 'I saw the glory of the God of Israel coming from the east. His voice was like the roar of rushing waters' (NIV). Jesus' divine authority is further revealed through the description in verse 16 that 'in his right hand he held seven stars'. Given the fact that seven is a number indicating completeness, we are being reminded that Jesus has the Church safely in his grasp. However, this is also a critique of the Roman Empire and a further reminder that it is God, not Domitian, who rules the world. Some time between AD77 and 81, Domitian's baby son died and was declared a god to be worshipped throughout the empire. On the back of Domitian-minted coins, there was an image of the emperor's son juggling seven stars to indicate his divine status, but John tells us here in verse 16 that it is actually Jesus Christ who holds the seven stars, not a Roman 'god'. Jesus Christ is the one with ultimate power and authority, not some pagan deity. We are not surprised to read, then, that Jesus speaks with divine authority: 'and coming out of his mouth was a sharp, double-edged sword' (NIV). The word of God that issues from the mouth of Christ is a word of judgment, but it is a double-edged sword. Some will hear his words and be set free; others will hear his words and be judged.

Finally in verse 16, we read, 'His face was like the sun shining in all its brilliance' (NIV). The disciple John had seen Jesus' face shine like the sun before, of course. If we go back to Matthew 17:1–9, we read the story of the transfiguration. Jesus led Peter, James and John up a high mountain and there 'he was transfigured before them. His face shone like the sun' (v. 2, NIV). On that occasion, Jesus spoke with Moses and Elijah, and the transfiguration story is a reminder that he is located within the line of Jewish prophets who announced the word of God to the world.

In these few verses from Revelation 1, then, we are given a profound vision of Christ. He is to be found in the midst of the churches and has royal authority. His work is completed and he has ascended to heaven. He is Judge of the world: nothing can escape his piercing gaze. He is Lord over heaven, earth and the Church; he comes to set us free as well as bringing judgment; he stands as a prophet to the nations. Here is an authority figure that demands and deserves the discipleship of young people.

However, we note that this a very different figure from the image that is often portrayed to young people today. We find it much easier to portray Jesus as 'best buddy' or 'mate'. We have often confused intimacy with informality and have encouraged the latter rather than the former. This is a travesty of the truth, which John does not allow for in Revelation and we should not encourage in Christian discipleship among Generation Y. We must not introduce young people to Jesus in such a way that they 'add him as a friend' to their life or click the 'like' button in response to his crucifixion, resurrection and ascension. There is an intimacy to be enjoyed with Jesus, to be sure, but this is not the same as informality. We serve Generation Y better by introducing them to a Saviour and Judge who is to be respected and adored rather than just another person within the flow of normal relationships. It may be a harder road to travel but it will result in deeper discipleship and stronger faith in the long term.

God the Holy Spirit

We noted that, in Revelation 1:4, the Holy Spirit was described as the seven spirits (or the sevenfold Spirit). This description is a clear indication of his divinity because it is a reflection of the Holy Spirit of God as prophesied in Isaiah 11. In verse 1 of that chapter, there is a prophecy of the coming of Christ: 'A shoot shall come out from the stump of Jesse, and a branch shall grow out of his roots.' Then, in verse 2, reference is made to the sevenfold activity of the Spirit of God with regard to the coming Messiah: 'The spirit of the Lord shall rest upon him, the spirit of wisdom and understanding, the spirit of counsel and might, the spirit of knowledge and the fear of the Lord.'

The sevenfold Holy Spirit prophesied in Isaiah 11 matches the notion of seven spirits in John's Revelation. The activities of the Holy Spirit listed there mark the characteristics we want to see developed in the young people we serve—the resting of God on their lives, wisdom, understanding, counsel, might, knowledge and fear of the Lord. Part of our task is to introduce them to the Holy Spirit and encourage them to receive his gifts. By so doing, we will be encouraging them to have their lives transformed by the Spirit of God, so that they may grow ever closer to the image of Christ.

While we want to encourage young people as spiritual beings, we must be careful to distinguish between subjective spirituality and the work of the Holy Spirit. All too often, that boundary becomes blurred in contemporary youth ministry. The intentions are good—the youth worker is desperate to encourage any sign of spiritual awareness within a young person—but it is unhelpful to the process of discipling if we claim too much for innate spirituality at the expense of a legitimate encounter with the Holy Spirit. John is very clear in Revelation that the Holy Spirit mediates the presence of God to the Church. That mediation results in a deeper intimacy with God the Father, accessed through the atoning work of God the Son. As Christians, we believe that innate spirituality remains barren unless it leads to a deepening love for God and a deepening awareness of his saving work. An authentic experience of the Holy Spirit is central to the life of discipleship. As Generation Y believers have an encounter with the Holy Spirit, so their faith will deepen and the church will strengthen. This is not to say that the old familiar forms of church will continue unabated, however. Clearly, we need to think afresh about how we 'do church' for this generation, and it is to this topic that we must now turn.

Some questions to consider

- What is your experience of God as Trinity? How might it transform your ministry to focus less on 'explaining' the Trinity and more on leading people into an experience of Trinity?
- How do your young people respond to the idea of God as their Father? Is this a positive image or a negative one? How might you re-present God as Father in such a way that they are attracted by the thought of sitting under his authority?
- How might you creatively engage your young people with the vision of Christ that John presents in Revelation 1:9–16?
- How do your young people respond when the idea of God as Judge is presented to them? How might we uphold this as a legitimate portrayal of God for Generation Y?
- To what extent do your young people relate to the Holy Spirit as a person rather than an energy force? How might you increase their knowledge and understanding in this matter?
- How might the sevenfold activity of the Spirit of God from Isaiah 11:2 impact the way in which you encourage young people to engage with the Holy Spirit?
- What gifts of the Spirit do you most long to see among the young people you work with? How might you best facilitate their engagement in this area of discipleship?

Chapter 3

What is the Church?

Generation Y: a sense of belonging

Contrary to popular opinion, the church offers exactly what young people are searching for. It may not be in a format that appears attractive to Generation Y but the underlying principle is absolutely perfect for this current generation.

'Belonging' is valued very highly by Generation Y. This is the most connected generation the world has ever known. Community is its heartbeat; relationship is the blood that pumps through the veins of this sociological cohort. It is probably the most widely researched social grouping in history, and, when exploring what is important to Generation Y, all the research across all the continents comes to exactly the same conclusion: family, friends, spouse, raising children and being happy with the right partner are in the top ten. Quite simply, Generation Y wants to 'belong'; it hungers for 'community'.

My frustration borders on anger when I hear older people complain that Generation Y is less willing to engage in 'community'. It is simply not true. Moreover, it is an unfair perception because it does not take into account the shifts in cultural patterns that have altered the practice of 'belonging' for Generation Y—shifts that have been forced on Generation Y by previous generations. For example, social mobility is stronger now than ever before. Families move home more regularly as parents pursue employment opportunities, making it difficult for young people to settle and engage. Increased divorce rates mean that many young people divide their time between the homes of two parents, having to forge two separate friendship groups to which they must try to 'belong'. Additionally, there is a heightened level of anxiety among parents of Generation Y children, which has resulted in the restriction of unsupervised activities beyond the home. Fear of terrorism, fear of paedophiles, fear of youth violence, fear of drugs, fear of physical safety as a result of increased numbers of cars and so on is the backdrop to many parenting decisions. As a result of these parental decisions, Generation Y is growing up with a greater degree of physical isolation than any generation before it. Given these shifts in social and cultural patterns, it is therefore unfair to expect Generation Y to engage in 'community' in the way that has been previously modelled.

Despite the legacy enforced on them by previous generations, there is an overwhelming desire among Generation Y to develop a sense of 'belonging', a sense of 'home'. Young people know that they develop a sense of identity through belonging. They know that they can only truly discover who they are when they are in relationship with others. For that reason, the church should be a natural place for young people to belong and discover their destiny in God. The church must be a community that welcomes Generation Y with open arms, willing both to learn and to teach. In so doing, however, there are three principles that must be embraced.

First, young people often discover who they are through something known as 'resistant identity'. This means that, in order to discover who they are, they must reject the patterns and norms of the wider culture and develop their own. That has been the history of youth culture since the word 'teenager' was invented in the 1950s, and it is worked out in two ways. There may be a wholesale rejection of the predominant culture. Young people may not want to sit through 'boring sermons' or 'dull services', wanting instead to discover new ways of worshipping God that swim against the local cultural tide. Alternatively, they may want to take existing cultural behaviours and adapt them for a new generation. We see this in the way that Generation Y has adopted both monastic and Celtic spiritual traditions and disciplines but reinterpreted them for a new age. However it manifests itself, the broader church must be willing to embrace the 'resistant identity' of Generation Y. It is not enough to expect young people to adopt existing patterns of 'doing church'. They must be given space to resist and find themselves with God in their own, unique way.

Second, the church must have realistic expectations of young people. I know of hardly any churches where the leadership pro-actively and positively educates the congregation in the cultural values of Generation Y. If the existing church members do not understand Generation Y norms, how can they be expected to embrace young people? The values of Generation Y will be mis-interpreted as 'lack of commitment', 'consumer Christianity', 'dis-respect', 'lack of staying power', 'selfishness' and worse. The church must strive to understand what motivates young people and how they view the world. As a result, their expectations will be realistic and churches will be able to absorb Generation Y Christians with grace and hospitality.

Third, the church must be willing to learn from Generation Y. I hope you will have noted already that this book is very positive about Generation Y! I sincerely believe that this generation has deep insights about God from which the rest of us can learn. Furthermore, it has the means and methodologies to access wis-dom and knowledge and deep community beyond anything the rest of us could ever have imagined. It is a humbling truth that the rest of us—the Silent Generation, the Baby Boomers and Generation X—must be prepared to sit at the feet of Generation Y and learn from them the deep mysteries of God. Of course, we have a great deal of acquired wisdom to share with young people—they know that and they are willing to learn—but there must be a reciprocal dialogue that I do not currently see replicated across local churches in general. Through dialogue and mutual learning, the church of God will be strengthened and the name of God will be glorified. It was the strengthening of the church and the glorification of God to which John was committed when he penned Revelation, and there are four fundamental truths explored by John that are at the very heart of a Generation Y experience of church.

Feeling part of something bigger

Unlike the rest of scripture (with the partial exception of Ephesians), the book of Revelation primarily emphasises the cosmic nature of the Church. As we read John's words, we are unable to escape from the idea that the Church transcends both time and space. There is no real division between the Church on earth and the Church in heaven, and there is no real division between the Church past, present or future. All is one in God. For Generation Y, which lives and breathes a technological revolution in which boundaries between space and time have been all but obliterated, this is a creative and exciting idea. When hosting youth activities for a small number of people, we are able to give them a sense of being part of something bigger. For Generation X and Baby Boomers, this has been a difficult tension to reconcile, but, for Generation Y, sitting in isolation in the bedroom in front of a screen that connects to the whole world, it really is not a problem.

In Revelation 4:1, John says, 'After this I looked, and behold a door standing open in heaven.'* Thereafter, he describes a scene of the Church united in heaven and on earth that is scarcely comprehensible in its magnitude. He begins his description in verse 4 by saying, 'Surrounding the throne were twenty-four other thrones, and seated on them were twenty-four elders. They were dressed in white and had crowns of gold on their heads' (NIV). In Revelation, we will come across two Greek words for 'crown'. The first is *stephanos*, which refers to the crown of victory given to the athlete who has run and won a race. The second is *diadem*, which refers to the crown worn by those in government who have authority over us. In 4:4, the reference is to a *stephanos* crown, indicating that the 24 elders are those who have run the spiritual race and received the crown as their reward. Their perseverance is reiterated by the fact that they wear white robes, which were the gift promised to the Christians in Sardis if they would stand firm in the faith (3:5). Similarly, the Laodiceans who persevered were promised a throne to sit on (3:21), which is mirrored in this verse.

Clearly, these 24 elders are the people of God who have persevered in the faith, overcome trials and temptations and remained faithful. They are the Church Triumphant. The fact that they number 24 in total is a reflection on 1 Chronicles 24—25. In 1 Chronicles 24:4 there are 24 elders called to carry out the priestly functions in the temple, and in 1 Chronicles 25 there are 24 elders chosen to look after the worship in the temple. Given the context of Revelation 4 and the activity of the 24 elders, the link is clear. This accords with 1 Peter 2:5, where Peter writes, 'You… are being built into a spiritual house to be a holy priesthood, offering spiritual sacrifices acceptable to God through Jesus Christ' (NIV).

Generation Y wants to be a part of a movement for change, a force for transformation. Young people are very happy to meet in small groups, as long as they can feel part of something bigger and more powerful. Those of us who are discipling them into the Christian faith have a responsibility to engage their imaginations creatively with the spiritual reality that is the Church united across space and time, both here and in eternity. Part of that discipling activity is to help them realise that they are the 24 elders seated on a throne, wearing a white robe on their body and a *stephanos* crown upon their head. Helping them to recognise this as their present reality and their eternal destiny will inform their decision-making and transform their relationship with God. It will also enable them to engage with the church here on earth, as represented by John elsewhere in Revelation.

A persecuted church

Being 'part of something bigger' is not necessarily good news, unfortunately. It is estimated that there were more Christian martyrs in the 20th century than in the previous 19 centuries added together. It is likely that the 21st century will see even more Christian martyrdoms than that. The stark reality facing Generation Y is that they will be asked by God to carry the mantle of the gospel in an increasingly hostile world. They may not seek out persecution but it is likely that persecution will, in some form, find them. For that reason, it is crucial that those of us engaged in discipling Generation Y help young people to be fully aware of, and engaged with, the persecuted church throughout the world. It must be a top priority in socialising young people into the Christian faith. In Revelation, John has much to say about 'the persecuted church'. For our purposes, we will focus on his teaching in chapter 9.

In verse 1, John writes, 'I saw a star that had fallen from heaven to earth, and he was given the key to the shaft of the abyss.'* Whether this star symbolises a human being or an angel is not of any real importance. What matters is the identity of 'the abyss', which is not a common biblical metaphor. When it is used, it is an idea that denotes the place of all that stands against God. There are allusions to 'the abyss' in Psalms, Isaiah and Amos. Furthermore, in Luke 8:31, when Jesus casts the spirits out of Legion, they beg him not to send them back into the abyss. Paul only uses the word once, in Romans 10:7: 'Who will descend into the abyss?' For him, it is the place of the dead. So here in Revelation 9, 'the abyss' represents all that stands against God and the life of his Church.

John tells us in verse 11 that '[the locusts] have as king over them the angel of the bottomless pit; his name in Hebrew is Abaddon'. This king, the angel of the abyss, therefore rules over all that stands against God and his Church. The Hebrew name Abaddon means 'Destruction' and, in Job 28:22, Abbadon and Death go hand in hand. So this is a king who is opposed to God and those who live in him, a king who brings destruction, a king who brings death.

John then makes the identity clear through a very clever word-play, saying, 'His name in Hebrew is Abaddon, and in Greek he is called Apollyon.' John knows very well that the Greek translation of Abaddon is not Apollyon! It is *apoleia*, a word that he uses in 17:8. However, instead of using the word *apoleia* here, he says 'Apollyon', which is derived from the name of the god Apollo. The worshippers of Apollo used the locust as one of their key symbols and, not surprisingly, the Emperor Domitian believed himself to be an incarnation of Apollo, so it seems that the locusts opposing and persecuting the Church of God are the Roman authorities. This passage is therefore a reference to the oppressive behaviour of political dictatorships. Their activities have an impact on the whole nation under their rule, and those who stand against them as a matter of faith and moral conscience will acutely feel their cruel responses.

Persecution and oppressive political activity are essentially demonic. In 9:2, John notes that 'from the shaft rose smoke like the smoke of a great furnace, and the sun and the air were darkened with the smoke from the shaft'. That which comes from the pit, from the place that opposes God, is toxic. We know from Ephesians 2:1–2 that the air was thought to be the place where demons lived, since Paul wrote there, 'You were dead through the trespasses and sins in which you once lived, following the course of this world, following the ruler of the power of the air, the spirit that is now at work among those who are disobedient.'

It is from this darkened, toxic, ungodly air that the locusts come: 'Then from the smoke came locusts on the earth' (9:3). The locust army from the abyss is released and scourges the world with its domination and oppressive rule. The nature of its oppressive activities, described in verses 5–10, is truly terrible—torture, violence, civil oppression and so forth. The impact is heartbreaking, as verse 6 reminds us: 'And in those days people will seek death but will not find it; they will long to die, but death will flee from them.' When we consider the brutality of oppressive regimes around the world today, our hearts break at the suffering the people endure, such that they think they would be better off dead than continuing to live under such cruelty. The ferocity of persecution and oppression is detailed in verse 5: '[The locusts] were allowed to torture them for five months.' A locust infestation normally lasts only a few days but the lifespan of a locust is five months. Therefore, John is saying that the whole existence, the *raison d'être*, of evil political regimes is focused on oppression and harm.

The church that Generation Y is inheriting will inevitably feel the force of the locust army to an increasing degree. It is not a pleasant message to pass on to young Christians. Nevertheless, it is an essential message for them to hear. We are being disingenuous if we do not warn them of the potential dangers of following Christ in this period of history.

The misunderstood church

Although it is not the case that every Generation Y Christian will face violent persecution, it is almost certainly the case that they will be misunderstood by the wider society and will therefore face some degree of marginalisation as a result of their faith in Jesus Christ. We are not surprised to learn that John has much to say about 'the misunderstood church' in Revelation.

In 2:8–11, John writes to the church in Smyrna. This was a prominent city in the Roman Empire, strategically positioned by the River Hermus to play a key role on the burgeoning trade route. There were many magnificent temples to pagan deities in Smyrna, not least to Athena and Roma, but there was also a strong Jewish population, out of which the church had grown. Smyrna was a magnificent, beautiful and wealthy city.

The message from God to the Christians there begins with the words, 'I know your afflictions and your poverty—yet you are still rich!' (2:9, NIV). Clearly, the Christians in Smyrna were suffering a great deal. The word that John uses here for 'poverty' is *ptocheian*, a very strong word referring to abject, extreme poverty. Yet, despite that abject poverty, they are still rich. We are reminded of Paul's words in 2 Corinthians 8:9: 'For you know the grace of our Lord Jesus Christ, that though he was rich, yet for your sake he became poor, so that you through his poverty might become rich' (NIV). Christ forsook his wealth and became poor for us, in order that he could take our poverty into himself on the cross and share his wealth with us. So John is reflecting Paul's words to the Corinthians here: 'I know your poverty—yet you are still rich!' We might suffer terribly in this life but we are rich in Christ. That being said, we must be careful not to spiritualise suffering too much. It is a betrayal of the gospel not to engage with issues of social justice and do what we can to alleviate the physical suffering of others. Jesus balances what he says here between the spiritual and the physical. He acknowledges their practical situation ('I know your poverty') but reminds them of their spiritual wealth ('yet you are still rich').

Getting to the heart of the situation, the reason for the Smyrnans' abject poverty is stated in Revelation 2:9: 'I know about the slander of those who say they are Jews and are not, but are a synagogue of Satan' (NIV). The Christians in Smyrna were not suffering from persecution under oppressive political behaviour by the Romans, as we considered above. Rather, they were being slandered and abused because of misunderstandings by the Jewish population in the city. Jewish aggression against the church was not untypical, of course. Paul faced it (we read of it in the Acts of the Apostles) and, throughout the next century, early Christian writers often comment on it. Furthermore, the Jewish authorities joined hands with the Romans in martyring Bishop Polycarp of Smyrna in AD155, re-portedly gathering the wood used to burn him at the stake, even though he was executed on a sabbath. Our reading of Revelation 2:9 is that a particular synagogue in Smyrna was slandering Christians in the city, telling lies about them to others, probably to the Roman authorities, so that they were finding it hard to get jobs, buy food, run businesses or participate in civil life. This slander by the Jews was causing economic hardship for the Christians. Christ does not promise them an early release from their suffering, but in verse 10 he says, 'Do not be afraid of what you are about to suffer' (NIV). Christ does not say for how long they will suffer but he does assure them that there is a reward waiting for them at the end—the *stephanos* crown of life.

This message to the Christians in Smyrna will increasingly be the message to Generation Y believers. Given the growing secularisation of our nation, they will be misunderstood, mocked and even marginalised as a result of standing firm in the faith. As the Generation Y church becomes ever more misunderstood, one of the most important spiritual qualities that we must nurture in our young people is patience, or perseverance. We must do all we can to encourage them to stand firm in the assurance that the *stephanos* crown of victory will be theirs.

The heavenly church

In the light of the difficulties mentioned above, it is crucial for us to do what we can to inspire Generation Y believers with a positive vision for their eternal future. This is exactly what John was seeking to achieve through his letter to the Christians in his spiritual care. He knew that they would be able to endure difficulties and misunderstandings only by placing them into an eternal context. He was not attempting to minimise their present suffering or to create a worldview that was in any sense escapist. Likewise, as we seek to inspire young people with a positive vision for their eternal destiny, we are not seeking to develop an escapist worldview that does not take seriously their present experiences of suffering or misunderstanding. On the contrary, we are helping them to understand their present in the context of God's future—the only reality that counts.

In Revelation 20:4, John has this incredible statement to make:

Then I saw thrones, and judgment was given for them who were seated on the thrones. I also saw the souls of those who had been beheaded *for their testimony to Jesus and for the worship of God. They had not worshipped the beast or its image and had not received its mark on their foreheads or their hands. They came to life and reigned with Christ a thousand years.**

Although there is some ambiguity in the Greek here (some versions translating the first sentence as 'Those seated on the thrones were given authority to judge', which I believe to be an erroneous reading), the idea of such final justification is rooted in Daniel 7:22: 'Judgment was given for the holy ones of the Most High.' Far from suggesting that the martyrs will cast judgment on the earth at the end times, John is stating that those who suffer persecution and marginalisation for the faith will be glorified in heaven as a reward for their faithfulness. This is a beautiful promise to share with young Christians, particularly those who are enduring mocking, bullying or misunderstanding as a result of their faith. Christ will be with them in their present trials and has a glorious future waiting for them if they persevere.

Being a Generation Y Christian is a difficult lifestyle to choose. We must do all we can to support and encourage those who are brave enough to swim against the contemporary tide in giving their lives over to Jesus. It is hard enough for young people to confess a faith in Christ, but it is harder still if they must then engage in a local church that is unwelcoming or reacts in passive-aggressive ways to their suggestions and enthusiasms. The church must rediscover the gift of hospitality to those people who see the world completely differently from the rest of us.

As well as being willing to welcome and learn from Generation Y, we must use our accumulated wisdom as spiritual elders to disciple young people effectively. In so doing, we will introduce them to a loving, gracious God with whom we find our happiness and fulfilment. However, we must also be honest enough to inform them of the spiritual battle in which they are engaged. They must fight against the world, the flesh and the devil. They readily understand the battle against the world, with its consumerist temptations and social injustice. They also understand the battle against the flesh—the continuous assault of the pursuit of happiness through physicality and readily accessible hedonism—but the battle against the devil is less easily grasped by a generation that has little experience of the Christian narrative. In our next chapter, we think in more detail about the spiritual warfare that John outlines in Revelation and how we can encourage a positive and proactive response among Generation Y believers.

Some questions to consider

- What do your young people think about the local church? How does the local church seek to be relevant for Generation Y? What can be done to improve the situation?
- What evidence do you have that the young people you work with want to 'belong'? How can your local church create an environment of hospitality and welcome, in which young people can truly 'belong'?
- What does 'resistant identity' look like among the young people you work with? How can it be embraced by the local church in such a way that the whole congregation learns from their practices?
- In what ways can you encourage a sense of belonging to an international family of faith among your young people?
- How might you foster a deeper awareness about, and engagement with, the persecuted church among your young people?
- In what ways are your Christian young people misunderstood for their faith? In what ways is it difficult for them to persevere in the faith in their school or college environment and in their homes? How might you best support them in their current trials?
- How can you creatively inspire your young people to embrace their eternal destiny in such a way that they are encouraged to persevere in the Christian faith?

- What encouragement do you need to persevere in your ministry? Where might you get that encouragement? How might you go about facilitating it?

Chapter 4

Who is Satan?

Generation Y: spirituality without religion

Recent research explodes the myth that Generation Y is developing 'pick 'n' mix' spirituality. Certainly young people show an interest in a broad range of spiritual expressions—Christianity, yoga, re-incarnation, ouija boards, tarot, angelology and so forth—but it is not common practice to amalgamate them into some sort of privatised cosmology. Instead, enquiry about the spiritual world normally happens only when the young person is faced with a crisis, such as the death of a friend or family member, a near-death experience and so on. In an ordinary day, young people are not nearly so spiritually inquisitive. This is not to suggest that young people are unspiritual. Belief in the supernatural is common across Generation Y. Young people are often interested in spiritual discussions and keen to debate a range of possible beliefs if a conversation is initiated with them, but this tends to remain conceptual outside the framework of crisis. Once the crisis has passed, interest often reverts to the conceptual.

For this reason, it is difficult to disciple young people into an appropriate awareness of spiritual warfare. It is not uncommon for the church to take one of two positions. First, the reality of spiritual warfare may be downplayed with young people for fear of 'turning them off' Christianity. Many youth workers believe that asking young people to engage with the issue of spiritual warfare is asking them to return to a naivety that is unappealing to Generation Y. Second, the extreme opposite position may be taken, which is to focus on spiritual warfare to an unhealthy degree. The young person is discipled to see evil everywhere, the influence of Satan being all-pervasive. Worship tends to focus on the victory of Christ on the cross over sin and the devil, and every day provides a fresh opportunity to overcome the power of darkness in the name of Jesus and claim ground for the kingdom of God. Like C.S. Lewis, who, in his *Screwtape Letters*, argued that the devil likes nothing more than either disinterest or unhealthy interest, I would suggest that both of these extremes are unhelpful in discipling Generation Y. Regarding the latter position, much emphasis is placed on certain passages in Revelation. However, it is a barbarisation of John's teaching to take this approach because, as we shall go on to see, he had no unhealthy interest in Satan. His concern in penning Revelation was to glorify God, not to focus our minds on the powers of darkness. Everything he has to say about Satan must be understood in that light.

The truth is that Generation Y has no problem with comprehending the existence of evil. Young people encounter it on a daily basis as they witness in (almost) real time the slaughter of innocents in the Middle East, the latest terrorist attack in Asia, the abuse of economic privilege in Europe, the latest school shooting in the United States, and so on. Generation Y does not need to be convinced that evil is real, but the reality of evil is not seen to be connected with the existence of Satan. Beyond the church, we are unlikely to find young people who attribute evil to the involvement of a spiritual being. Satan has been reduced to a myth or, at most, a metaphor. There is a real challenge for the church to address this issue with Generation Y. With those who have not yet come to faith, the church must be courageous enough to find ways to engage them with the possibility and potentiality of negative spiritual forces. For those who have come to faith, the Church must undertake responsible discipling, encouraging a balanced perspective so that young Christians may find assurance and the conquest of anxiety. The teaching of John in Revelation helps us to address these issues and find that balance in a suitable manner.

The identity of Satan

The names 'Devil' and 'Satan' mean approximately the same thing: 'Adversary'. 'Devil' is derived from a Greek word and 'Satan' is derived from a Hebrew word. There is no single biblical idea of who Satan is. As the canon of scripture came together over a period of hundreds of years, so ideas about the origin and nature of Satan developed. It is true to say, however, that much of what is currently taught in our churches is not based on the biblical evidence but on poetic ideas and extra-biblical narratives that arose after the early Christian writings.

Old Testament teaching about Satan is ambiguous. The word 'satan' there does not have the connotations that we attach to it now, because it can refer to a human adversary as much as to a spiritual adversary. For example, in 1 Kings 11:14 and 23, God raises up an adversary ('satan') against Solomon. The Philistines use the same word to describe David in 1 Samuel 29. Even when angels are described as adversaries (or 'satans') in the Old Testament, it is not necessarily a derogatory idea. In Numbers 22:22, we read, 'God was angry because Balaam was going, and as he came riding on his donkey, accompanied by his two servants, the angel of the Lord took his stand in the road to bar his way.' The word used here concerning the angel of the Lord is 'adversary'. Contrary to popular opinion, there is no explicit teaching about the fall of Satan in the Old Testament.

As time went by, the word *satan* became specifically attached to the spirit that we think of today. Even so, there is a broad range of ideas about this spirit in scripture. When he is mentioned in Job and Zechariah, Satan does not have any authority of his own but is subordinate to God. In the New Testament, God uses Satan to inflict suffering or punishment (1 Corinthians 5:5). Satan hinders the progress of the gospel (1 Thessalonians 2:18). He is an accuser but he is not a fighter: resist him and he will flee (James 4:7). He may wander around like a roaring lion (1 Peter 5:8) but his works have been destroyed (1 John 3:8) and his time is limited (Revelation 12:12).

Although we do not want to give Satan more attention than he is worth, we do have a responsibility in our discipling of Generation Y to inform young people about the adversary they face. We must educate responsibly and biblically, which is why the teaching from Revelation is so useful and important for our purposes. In essence, John's teaching about Satan is very simple, with two primary strands of thought. First, Satan has not been able to destroy Christ, so he wants to destroy his Church. Second, the work of Satan has been defeated already on the cross and his end will soon come. We now consider each of these ideas in turn.

Satan and the Church

There is much written about Satan in Revelation, but the primary teaching about his attempts to destroy the Church is in chapter 12. Although we may be taken aback or even fearful when we read this chapter, it is important to note that John based it on a popular story from the period that was told in various formats throughout the Middle East. Here are a few examples.

- There was a Greek myth about the birth of the god Apollo from the goddess Leto and the great dragon, called Python, who realised that he would be killed by Apollo. Python pursued Leto to kill her, but she was carried off to Poseidon. When the child Apollo grew strong, he slew the dragon.
- There was an Ugaritic myth, in which the god Ba'al battled against Yam, the prince of the sea. Ba'al defeated the sea-monster and set up his kingdom's rule.

- There was an Akkadian myth in which Tiamat, a seven-headed dragon, threatened war against the gods and drew down a third of the stars. Marduk, the god of light, slew the dragon.
- There was an Egyptian myth in which the goddess Isis gave birth to the god Horus. The dragon Typhon pursued Isis to kill her but she escaped to the island of Chemnis. When Horus grew strong enough, he killed the dragon.
- There was a Zend myth, in Persia, in which the fire god fought the dragon Azhi Dahaka. The dragon threw a third of the stars on to the earth before being slain.

From these examples, we realise that Revelation 12 is based on an ancient myth that was common currency in the Middle East. As we saw in Chapter 1 of this book, John is not portraying literal events but teaching spiritual truths. He is using a popular story to explain a truth about God's victory over Satan in much the same way that, in his parables, Jesus used contemporary-based stories to teach truths about God. If we remember its context as we work through the detail of the passage, we can find chapter 12 useful in our efforts to disciple Generation Y.

John begins his telling of the story in verse 1 with the statement, 'A great sign appeared in the sky: a woman clothed with the sun, with the moon under her feet, and on her head was a crown of twelve stars.'* The woman represents the Church, which, in verse 2, is 'pregnant and... crying out in birth pangs, in the agony of giving birth'. This picture draws on an Old Testament image of the people of God in labour, found in Isaiah 26:17–18:

As a woman with child and about to give birth writhes and cries out in her pain, so were we in your presence, O Lord. We were with child and we writhed in pain, but we gave birth to wind. We have not brought salvation to the earth; we have not given birth to people of the world. *

The old Israel could not give birth to salvation but the new Israel, the Church, could do so because Christ is, in a sense, born in us and dwells among us. Thus, for John, the Church is suffering the pangs of giving birth to the Messiah through its missional activity.

In verse 3, however, we read that 'another sign appeared in the sky: a great red dragon, with seven heads and ten horns, and seven diadems on his heads'.* This is a description of Tiamat from the Akkadian myth, who is the great enemy of heaven. For John, this red dragon represents all that is antichrist on earth, standing in defiance against God. It wears seven crowns on its head, but the Greek word used here for 'crown' is not *stephanos*, the crown of victory. Instead, it is *diadem*, which in this case represents a claim to authority in opposition to God.

Verse 4 says, 'His tail swept down a third of the stars of heaven and threw them to the earth. Then the dragon stood before the woman who was about to bear a child, so that he might devour her child as soon as it was born.' Some people take this verse to mean that Satan was an angel who fell from heaven and took a third of the angels with him, but there is no reason to read that interpretation into the text. It does not fit with the fact that this is a common mythological picture; nor does it fit with the other usages of the proportion 'a third' in Revelation. Instead, John is merely emphasising that the evil of satanic oppression has a sizeable impact on the world, but it is still limited—a third only.

In verse 5, we read that 'she gave birth to a son, a male child, who is to rule all the nations with a rod of iron'. Here, we are drawn back to Psalm 2:8–9, where the coming Messiah is described in this way by God: 'I shall give you nations as your domain... You will break them with a rod of iron.'* But in the same verse we encounter the interesting idea that 'her child was snatched away and taken to God and to his throne'. John is stating that the whole Christ-event, from his birth in Bethlehem to his ascension outside Jerusalem, is the root of our salvation. It is through the whole life and ministry of Jesus that we are saved.

Then we are told that 'the woman fled into the wilderness, where she has a place prepared by God, so that there she can be nourished' (v. 6). Jewish history is peppered with stories about Israel seeking sanctuary in the wilderness and, while there, enjoying God's provision for them. Similarly, in these last days between the ascension and the second coming of Jesus, the church is in a wilderness experience with God, enjoying his protection and provision. We can therefore be reassured and comforted by God's protection before reading the horror of verses 7–9:

And war broke out in heaven; Michael and his angels fought against the dragon. The dragon and his angels fought back, but they were defeated, and there was no longer any place for them in heaven. The great dragon was thrown down, that ancient serpent, who is called the Devil and Satan, the deceiver of the whole world – he was thrown down to the earth, and his angels were thrown down with him.

It is in his defeat that Satan is named. The dragon is the ancient serpent, bringing to mind the story of Genesis 3, where deceit was performed on Adam and Eve, the first people of God. The dragon is the Devil and Satan, the deceiver of the whole world.

Having been unable to defeat Christ, this is the point in John's story where Satan turns his rabid attention to the Church: 'So when the dragon saw that he had been thrown down to the earth, he pursued the woman who had given birth to the male child' (v. 13). If he cannot defeat the Saviour, then he will attempt to defeat the people of God instead. However, John gives further assurance as to the futility of Satan's attempts in verse 14: 'But the woman was given the two wings of the great eagle, so that she could fly from the serpent into the wilderness, to her place where she is nourished.' No matter how much Satan seeks to destroy and harm, the Church remains safe in its wilderness resting-place with God. This is not to say that we can be complacent about Satan, because, as John reminds us in verse 17, 'the dragon was angry with the woman, and went off to make war on the rest of her children, those who keep the commandments of God and hold the testimony of

Jesus'. Satan is at war with all Christians: that is a fact. The angels have frustrated him, the Redeemer has defeated him, he has lost his place in heaven and so he vents his rage on us. That is the way of the world until the second coming and his final vanquishing.

As we disciple Generation Y, we must be sure to inform young people about the reality of Satan. However, following John's lead in Revelation, we must neither succumb to sensationalist ideas nor give more credit to Satan than he is due. Yes, Satan attacks; yes, Satan vents his anger at us; but the Church is secure in the provision and protection of God. The Redeemer has defeated Satan. Believers have nothing to fear and we are told in verse 12, 'Rejoice then, you heavens and those who dwell in them!' The battle is not over but the war has been won, and that is the truth in which young people must be encouraged to stand.

The end of Satan

The final defeat of Satan is outlined in Revelation 20, which has proven to be one of the most divisive of all passages in scripture. Interpretations vary from the academically stringent to the ridiculously populist. In truth, it is a difficult portion of scripture to understand and we should approach it with deep humility. However, even though we acknowledge differences of interpretation concerning the detail, the broad sweep of John's intent is clear.

When it comes to discipling Generation Y, we must be sure to dispel the myth held by many that there is a battle raging between God and Satan. That is just not true. In 20:1–2, John tells us, 'I saw an angel coming down from heaven, holding in his hand the key to the bottomless pit and a great chain. He seized the dragon, that ancient serpent, who is the Devil and Satan, and bound him for a thousand years.' John is stressing the fact that Satan is not very powerful. It does not take Almighty God to bind him; an angel is perfectly capable of the task. We must not encourage young people to harbour ideas that overplay the power of Satan and speak of him as if he were a worthy adversary of God. He is not. Satan is bound by an angel and thrown into a sealed pit for 1000 years so that he is unable to deceive the nations.

There is, of course, much debate about what this period of 1000 years represents in John's thought. Some believe that Jesus will return, the Christian dead will be raised and they will reign together on earth for 1000 years before a brief release of Satan heralds the final judgment. Others believe that the 1000 years symbolises a 'golden age' of Christian mission and human development that precedes the return of Christ and the final judgment. Still others believe that the 1000 years is purely symbolic, a metaphor to describe the period of history between the first coming of Jesus and the second coming.

It is not the intention of this book to promote one reading of the text over another. We must each come to our own conclusions about the nature of the millennial period. However, it may be helpful to note that, just as John drew on ancient myths from around the Middle East to draw a picture for us in Revelation 12, so he does the same here with regard to the binding of Satan for a period of time. For example, the Persian Zend religion has a story in which the wicked serpent Azi-Dahaka is overcome by Thraetaeona and chained in a mountain for 9000 years. There are similar stories in the Egyptian myth of Osiris and in later Mandaean traditions, as well as Scandinavian and Germanic folk religions. Jewish writings such as Enoch and the Prayer of Manasseh follow a similar theme without being explicit concerning a millennium. The closest Old Testament parallel is Isaiah 24:21–22, where we read, 'On that day the Lord will punish the host of heaven, in heaven, and the kings of the earth, on earth. They will be gathered together as prisoners in a pit; they will be shut up in a prison, and after many days they will be punished.'* While there may be debate over John's exact meaning, it seems clear that he is again dealing in metaphor and myth to reveal a deeper spiritual truth.

More crucial, however, is John's comment in 20:3: 'After that, he must be let out for a little while.' This, of course, begs the question, if Satan has been bound, why must he be let out again? At the heart of the answer is the small word 'must' or, in Greek, *dei*, which literally means 'it is necessary'. The release of Satan from the pit is integral to the plan of God for salvation. Satan does not escape, and he is not bounced out of his prison by demons. Rather, 'it is necessary' for God to release him for a short while in order to achieve the salvation of the world. God has absolute authority over Satan. John concludes the story of Satan's fate in verse 10 by stating that, after the final rebellion, he is cast into the lake of fire and sulphur where his torment will never end.

The Christian assurance

Many young Christians live in fear of Satan, too heavily influenced by populist and sensationalist ideas that have little or nothing to do with coherent biblical interpretation. It is absolutely crucial that those of us involved in discipling Generation Y disabuse them of erroneous doctrines and encourage them into a balanced and coherent perspective. We must contextualise an understanding of Satan within the notion of Christian assurance, based on the authority and power of God. There are four points to consider briefly in this regard.

First, we must help young people to understand that God is the real object of Satan's anger. We do not want anyone to labour under the conviction that 'Satan is out to get me'. He is not. Quite simply, he wants to get at God. Certainly, he uses each one of us in his game plan but we are not the direct object of his fury. In Revelation 20:8, Satan gathers the enemies of God at Gog and Magog. We read in verse 9 that these enemies 'surrounded the camp of the saints and the beloved city'. There is a lovely nuance in this verse that brings together the whole history of Israel to this point in time. First, John mentions 'the camp of the saints', which draws our mind back to the early Israelites as pilgrims of God wandering in exile, waiting to enter the promised land. Then he mentions 'the beloved city', which is a reference to the settled period of Israelite history when the city of Jerusalem was built around the temple. So the whole of the history of the people of faith is represented here in nine short words. Because Israelite history is summed up in this verse, it is clear that the attack at Gog and Magog is not directed solely against the Church but against the purposes of God throughout all history. This is an attack on God himself, through his people. As such, the attack is doomed to fail and we can encourage young people to take real assurance in that fact.

Second, we must convince young people that Satan can never force them into sin. They are not helpless marionettes in the hand of an evil spirit that pulls their strings and makes them dance. In 20:10, Satan is described as the one 'who had deceived them'. What is clear here, and what we need to remember, is that the Devil is not the originator, source or creator of sin. All the Devil does is to work on the sinful possibilities that are inherent within each of us. In this passage, it is the armies of Gog and Magog that have within them the possibility of sin. The Devil just comes along and plays on their weakness, deceiving them. Therefore, we have no excuse to join with Adam and Eve and blame the serpent for our sin. We are solely responsible for our own sins and cannot pass the buck to Satan. His only role in our sinfulness is to tempt and deceive us, to strengthen our will to sin, but never to create sin in us in the first place. He is not that powerful. While that means young people must accept responsibility for their own actions, it also means that they can be liberated from the fear of being controlled by Satan. That liberation is at the very heart of Christian assurance.

Third, young people need to know that Satan cannot ultimately affect the course of history. To be sure, satanic oppression causes very real tragedies but the final authority over history remains with God. As we shall see in the next chapter, the history of the world is written on a scroll and is in the hand of God in heaven

(Revelation 5). We learnt from 12:8 that Satan has been cast out of heaven, so he cannot permanently affect the course of history. God is sovereign and it is the Lamb, not Satan, who opens the scroll. Generation Y is growing up in very uncertain and fearful times. In discipling young people, we must seek to assure them that God is in control and Satan sits under his authority.

Fourth, and crucially, young people need to know that Satan can no longer act as their accuser. Quite simply, he cannot accuse us before God because he is no longer in God's presence. In 12:10, John tells us:

I heard a loud voice in heaven proclaiming, 'Now have come the salvation and the power and the kingdom of our God and the authority of the Messiah, for the accuser of our comrades has been thrown down, who accuses them day and night before our God.'

The more we reflect on that fact, the more amazing it becomes to us. We no longer stand accused before God because of our sin, because there is no one in heaven to accuse us. We are completely free from guilt because Christ has made us righteous, and there is no one in heaven to tell God any different. Young people so often labour under a conviction of guilt and shame and, as a result, feel unworthy before God. However, a central factor in the assurance of their salvation is the fact that Satan has been cast out of heaven and cannot accuse us before God.

The good news for Generation Y, and for all of us, is contained in 12:11: 'But they have conquered him by the blood of the Lamb and by the word of their testimony.' This is why Satan has been defeated. This is why there is no hope of Satan ever regaining control or victory. His defeat has come as a result of the blood of the Lamb. This verse is a brilliant counterpoint to 12:7: there, Michael fights Satan—but the victory is not won by the angelic host. It is the Son of God who, having died, been raised and ascended into heaven, has won the victory. That is why our salvation is secure and that is the good news that we must share with Generation Y.

Some questions to consider

- What has been your previous understanding about the nature of Satan? How has that changed now?
- What do your young people think about Satan? What images are there in youth cultures that make for a healthy understanding? What images and ideas make for an unhealthy understanding?
- In what ways do you see Satan attacking God through the church in your current situation?
- In what ways do your young people feel accused before God? How might you help them to have a more healthy perspective?
- How might you help young people to understand that God, not Satan, is in control of the course of human history?

Chapter 5

How do I understand suffering in the world?

Generation Y: global awareness and the experience of pain

Early analysis of Generation Y led commentators to suggest that it was the most cosseted and comfortable generation in history. I would suggest that the course of global events and cultural shifts since the beginning of the current millennium should result in a reassessment of this view. I would not want to argue that Generation Y has experienced suffering to the same degree as the Silent Generation. Living through the wars and economic depression of the first half of the 20th century is an experience that we would not wish on anyone. However, I would argue that not only does this current generation know what it is to suffer but it is also, through social media, witness to global suffering in an unprecedented manner. For that reason, Generation Y legitimately questions the existence of God in a world that seems content to allow tremendous suffering to continue, despite having the resources to end much of it. In discipling Generation Y, we must have a coherent response to this issue.

As a result of both the experience and the witness of suffering, Generation Y is negatively affected. On a daily basis, either through the screen or in real time, young people encounter global terrorism and civil wars, ecological disasters, the fallout of dysfunctional family relationships, civil violence, aggression and problems related to debt and economic failure. Due to the protected nature of their upbringing, young people are often ill-equipped to know how to respond to such experiences, and this results in heightened levels of anxiety. In *The Courage to Be*, Paul Tillich identified three primary forms of anxiety: ontic anxiety (a preoccupation with death), personal guilt, and spiritual anxiety (emptiness and loss of meaning). He noted that anxiety reaches heightened levels at the end or beginning of an era because there is a conflict between old and new that results in the apprehension of transition. It is not surprising, then, that Generation Y, which has a worldview so profoundly different from what has come before, should experience heightened anxieties in each of the three ways identified by Tillich.

To date, the church has not been very successful in meeting the anxieties of Generation Y. We have clung to forms of worship that bring comfort to the Silent Generation and Baby Boomers, more through nostalgia than content. We intercede for the world in ways that are politically neutral so as not to cause upset or division in the congregation. We speak of spiritual poverty without addressing material need, we preach a gospel of reconciliation without being proactive where there is societal rupture, and we pray for peace without holding our politicians accountable for violence. Generation Y is smart. Young believers are quick to recognise the emptiness of our efforts and denounce our hypocrisy and inactivity. Generation Y wants to change the world, and will do it with or without the church. As Christians, we believe that the gospel provides a valuable insight into pain and suffering, but unless we are willing to be bolder, Generation Y will bypass the church and seek answers elsewhere. It is for this reason that we do well to rediscover John's teaching on the subject in Revelation.

The context of suffering in Revelation

As we consider John's teaching, we must begin with a series of disclaimers. We will be focusing in part on Revelation 6 as we consider the reality of suffering in the world and what our response to it should be. However, it is absolutely crucial that we understand what is *not* being said before we try to discern what *is* being said. Here are four disclaimers to inform our study.

First, Revelation 6 details the opening of the seals of the scroll. The scroll is the detail of the course of history, which God holds in his hand. As the scroll is opened, the seven seals are broken. Each seal represents a different judgment of God on the world—but we must be clear about two points in this regard. The judgments revealed through the seals are not the same as the final judgment, which will be explored in a later chapter; and these judgments need to be understood as consequences in a fallen world. It is not being suggested that God is the author of war, famine, death, disease and so on, but God can use these consequences of a fallen world to issue judgments. To reiterate, there is a huge difference between seeing God as the author of suffering and understanding that God can use suffering to warn and to judge. Since we believe in a God who is, by definition, good and loving, we must be absolutely sure to recognise the difference.

Second, John is not arguing that all suffering in the world must be seen as a judgment from God. It was not part of his purpose in penning Revelation to provide a comprehensive analysis of the cause of suffering in the world. The truth is that sometimes suffering just happens and we must not try to 'find God in it', far less look for a judgment or warning. We live in a fallen world in which there is much experience of pain. We are not encouraged by Revelation to theologise all such experiences. John is making a general point about how God is able, if he wishes, to use the experience of suffering to bring about a judgment or warning.

Third, when we read of these judgments in Revelation 6, we must be absolutely clear that they are judgments on the world, not judgments specifically related to individuals. This is a crucial point because so many Christians have misunderstood and thereby developed harsh, judgmental theologies. For example, some might have seen the 2011 tsunami and earthquake in Japan and believed it to be God's judgment on Buddhists or Shintoists. Some time ago, when HIV-AIDS was first discovered, some Christians proclaimed it as God's judgment on the gay community. Others will look at civil disorder in the Middle East and see it as God's judgment on Muslims. Others may look at areas of famine in the world and believe that God is judging the victims for some kind of sin. That is not what Revelation 6 is saying! These are not individual judgments wrought by God on individual people. It is a description of the fallen nature of God's good creation—and, through the consequences of the fall, we gain a sense of God's displeasure at sin. God does not send war or famine or plague to punish individuals. These types of event are a result of the fallen nature of the world and, by definition, contain within them a judgment on fallenness.

Fourth, the opening of the seals is not in any sense chronological. Some Christians have tried to plot the history of the world through the opening of the seals in an attempt to determine when the second coming will happen. So, for example, the first seal indicates the rise of the Parthians, the fourth seal indicates the bubonic plague, the fifth seal indicates martyrdom under Communist regimes, the sixth seal indicates global warming and so on. This is a mistaken approach. All the seals are happening at one and the same time and we need to read them only as signs of the age.

Revelation 6, which is deeply rooted in Old Testament imagery and paralleled in Mark 13, is outlining the reality that there will be judgments on a fallen world before the consummation of the kingdom of God. These judgments will take a number of different forms, as we explore below.

International disorder

The identity of the rider on the white horse in verse 2 has long been open to debate. Many have taken him to represent Christ. Those who take this interpretation point to the fact that the white horse could represent purity, the rider is wearing a *stephanos* crown, and he goes forth to conquer. However, such an interpretation is not without its difficulties, not least because Jesus has already been identified in verse 1 as the Lamb who opens the seal. It is difficult to see how he could be both Lamb and rider. It is perhaps easier to identify the rider as a generalised statement about nations that conquer in warfare. Certainly, in Mark 13:8, when Jesus is talking about the end times, he warns that 'nation will rise against nation, and kingdom against kingdom'. This is therefore a very plausible interpretation, especially as the rider carries a bow, which is a weapon of war.

As we mentioned above, this is not to say that God causes or rejoices in international conflict but only that he can use such behaviour to issue warnings or judgment. We see the same idea in the Old Testament, particularly through the writings of the prophets who see the conquering of Israel and Judah by other nations as judgment for infidelity to their calling as the chosen people of God. God does not rejoice in the vanquishing of nations and untimely deaths caused by war but he is able to use that human activity as a means of bringing his own judgment to bear.

Civil disorder

In Revelation 6:3–4, a red horse appears with a rider 'permitted to take peace from the earth, so that people would slaughter one another; and he was given a great sword'. The horse is red, which signifies bloodshed, but a clue is given as to the specific nature of this violence through the use of two words, 'sword' and 'slaughter'. In 1:16, the double-edged sword that issues from Jesus' mouth is a broadsword used in battle, indicated by the use of the word *romphaia*. Here, however, a different type of sword is indicated by the use of the word *machaira*. This was a short Roman sword, used by civil authorities to execute rebels. Similarly, a rather specific word is used for 'slaughter'. Derived from the Greek word *sphadzo*, it relates primarily to the butchering of people in a particularly violent way.

What is being portrayed here is the violence of internal strife, civil wars in which people attack and slay one another. In Mark 13:12, Jesus warns about this type of behaviour as a sign of the times: 'Brother will betray brother to death, and a father his child. Children will rebel against their parents and have them put to death' (NIV). Although God is not the instigator of such violence, which is ultimately a result of fallen human nature, he is able to use these situations as judgments on our broken world.

Economic disorder

In verses 5–6, a black horse appears, with its rider holding scales in his hand and proclaiming, 'A quart of wheat for a day's pay, and three quarts of barley for a day's pay, but do not damage the olive oil and the wine!' In accordance with Jesus' prophecy in Mark 13:8, this represents famines that come upon the earth. The fact that the rider has scales in his hand suggests that food will be rationed and carefully weighed out. In Leviticus 26:26, God says, 'When I cut off your supply of bread, ten women will be able to bake your bread in one oven, and they will dole out the bread by weight. You will eat, but you will not be satisfied' (NIV). Again in Ezekiel 4:16–17, God says, 'I am about to cut off the food supply in Jerusalem. The people will eat rationed food in anxiety and drink rationed water in despair, for food and water will be scarce' (NIV). With regard to the quantities, a quart of wheat was deemed necessary for a working man to eat each day, so here is a day's wages for one day's food for one man. All that would be left for his family is inferior barley. Even three quarts for a day's wages would be a starvation diet for them all.

Alarmingly, we note the command, 'Do not harm the olive oil and the wine.' Upon consideration, it becomes clear that this is the experience of many in the world who suffer the ravages of hunger and starvation. Even in times of famine, there are those in authority and with great wealth who manage to continue enjoying the luxuries of life. We have seen such sickening scenes recently:

the living conditions of the people of Zimbabwe in contrast with those of Robert Mugabe, the wealth of Saddam Hussein's palaces and feasts while his people were starving, and the continued wealth and comfort of President Assad while the people of Syria struggled to survive. Wheat is unaffordable, barley is unaffordable, but the oil and the wine remain unaffected. This is part of the evil of the fall.

Disease and pestilence

It is slightly strange that the rider of the horse in verses 7–8 is named as Death in most translations of the Bible, given the fact that all the seals can result in death befalling humanity. The word for 'death', *thanatos*, is sometimes used in the Greek translation of the Old Testament to mean 'pestilence' or 'plague' (see, for example, Ezekiel 14:21), and that is probably John's meaning here. This accords, again, with the prophecy of Jesus in Mark 13:8, where he states, 'There will be great earthquakes, famines and pestilences in various places.'* It is only natural, of course, for Hades to follow close behind the pestilence as people die and are condemned to the netherworld in Jewish belief.

Disorder in creation

The story of the fall in Genesis 3 implies cosmic consequences. It is not just human beings who carry within their DNA the impact of turning away from God. The whole created order is negatively affected. As a result of the humans' choice, animals are cursed (v. 14), enmity enters the world (v. 15), pain becomes part of the process of creation (v. 16) and the very ground itself is cursed (v. 17). As Paul reminds us in Romans 8:21, part of the process of salvation is that 'the creation itself will be set free from its bondage to decay'.

For that reason, we are not surprised to learn from Revelation that the created order contains within it an inherent disposition to wreak havoc and cause suffering. When the sixth seal is opened in 6:12–13, there are consequences for creation: 'There came a great earthquake; the sky became black as sackcloth; the full moon became like blood, and the stars of the sky fell to the earth.' Here we see a symbolic enactment of Jesus' prophecy in Mark 13:8, 24–25. As Jesus goes on to warn in 13:28–29, 'Now learn this lesson from the fig-tree: As soon as its twigs get tender and its leaves come out, you know that summer is near. Even so, when you see these things happening, you know that it is near, right at the door' (NIV). A disordered creation is a sign of the times.

Forging a response to the problem of suffering

The nature of the world between the first coming and the second coming of Christ is described in the opening of these seals. There are wars, there is civil disorder, there is famine, there is pestilence and there is chaos in the created order. We learn how God may use these consequences of the fall to issue judgments on or warnings to human civilisation. Given the stark reality of a disordered creation, we are not surprised to read in Revelation 6:15 of people hiding in caves and among the rocks of the mountains, trying to escape the judgment of God. Again, this accords with Jesus' prophecy recorded in Mark 13:14: 'When you see the "abomination that causes desolation" standing where it does not belong... then let those who are in Judea flee to the mountains' (NIV). Neither are we surprised that, in Revelation 6:15, John lists seven categories of people who try to flee from the judgment of God: 'the kings of the earth, the princes, the generals, the rich, the mighty, and everyone else, both slave and free' (NIV). The whole human race tries to avoid judgment; the whole human race tries to hide from God.

It seems that we have learnt nothing from the poor example of Adam and Eve, who tried to hide from God in Genesis 3:8. They hid because they were ashamed of their nakedness. Even in the last days, all humanity will be ashamed of its spiritual nakedness and will again try to hide from God. As we seek to disciple Generation Y, however, we must forge in them a better response to the judgment of God inherent in some experiences of global suffering. It is not enough for us to let them run and hide. We want them to face God with confidence and so we must instil in them a robust theological understanding. There are three ideas that will help them grow into such maturity.

First, we will encourage our young people to see these global sufferings for what they are—the consequences of a fallen world that may contain within them judgments and warnings from God. As such, these events still sit under the sovereignty of God and are within his ultimate control. Describing the chaos of malignant destruction in Revelation 9:14, John records a voice saying, 'Release the four angels who are bound at the great river Euphrates' (NIV). The fact that these angels have hitherto been bound suggests that God has limited them and restricted their activities. Furthermore, in 9:15 we read that 'the four angels were released, who had been held ready for the hour, the day, the month, and the year, to kill a third of humankind'. This verse again tells us about the authority of God. The angels have 'been held ready', which indicates that they are tied to a specific, preordained moment of God's choosing. In addition, they kill only 'a third of humankind'. This is a sizeable minority, to be sure, but a limited number all the same. Even in this chaotic moment, God is still sovereign and still Lord of all. We must enable our young people to comprehend God's sovereignty even in the midst of what appears to be a chaotic world order.

Second, we will encourage our young people to persevere in faith, even in the midst of their own personal experiences of suffering. The church at Thyatira, which received a personal message from Christ in Revelation 2:18–29, knew what it was to suffer. In his compassion, Jesus commends them in 2:19 with words that have been translated from the Greek as, 'I know your deeds, your love and faith, your service and perseverance, and that you are now doing more than you did at first' (NIV). However, the nuance of the original Greek is important, where it says literally, 'I know your deeds and your love and your faith and your perseverance, and your works the last greater than the first.' Rather than saying that the Thyatirans are now doing more than they did at first, Jesus is actually commending them for their deeds, love, faith, service and perseverance but saying that the last of these, their perseverance, is more valuable than the first of these, their deeds. He is saying that the situation in which they find themselves is really difficult and he commends them, above all else, for their perseverance. We know that our young people often face considerable struggles in their personal lives. This commendation from Christ assures them that perseverance is an admirable spiritual quality to have. Sometimes, it is as much as we can do to hold on, to hang on in there, despite our personal pain. Jesus commends our young people for persevering through tough times. In fact, 2:19 assures them that Jesus is more pleased with their perseverance than any engagement in Christian activity they may feel obliged to undertake.

Third, we will encourage our young people to pray. In 6:10, the martyrs cry out, 'Sovereign Lord, holy and true, how long will it be before you judge and avenge our blood on the inhabitants of the earth?' We will be considering this verse in more detail in a subsequent chapter. However, it is enough at this stage to note that the martyrs are interceding for God's justice to come upon earth. As we disciple Generation Y, we must encourage them to develop as a people of prayer, a people of intercession, who will remember before God those who suffer and ask for the righteousness of God to be revealed among the nations.

Interpreting the pain

In his book *Israel's Praise*, Walter Brueggemann suggested that 'all true theology begins in pain'. It is certainly the case that we grow closer to God through times of trial than in moments of happiness. It is when we encounter suffering that we are forced to ask the most difficult questions of ourselves, of others and of God. We do not court suffering, nor do we pray that God would inflict pain on us in order that we may develop spiritually; but when we suffer, or when we see the suffering of others, a door is opened to us through which we may pass into a deeper relationship with God. That, of course, was John's testimony in Revelation. He was in exile on Patmos, separated from those he loved because of his faith, but in his loneliness and isolation he met with God in the most profound of ways and was able to share that experience with believers in each and every century. In the midst of his suffering he entered the mystery of God and was able to finish his letter (contrary to many English translations) with the great proclamation, 'The grace of the Lord Jesus with all' (22:21). It was only through contemplation of his own suffering and constant intercession for his suffering flock that he was able to come to such a deep awareness of the omnipresence of God.

Central to the task of discipling Generation Y is to help them not just to survive pain but to interpret it. This is not the same as the naïve response that seeks to find God in each and every moment of suffering. The testimony of Revelation and the history of the early church do not attest to that. The interpretation of pain is reliant upon the view expressed by Paul in Romans 8:28: 'We know that for those who love God, all things work together towards good.'* Far from encouraging us to find God in each separate experience of suffering, Paul suggests that we take the long view: the 'good' to which he refers is our eternal destiny with God. Paul is not saying that the 'good' is in each moment of suffering but that even our moments of suffering contribute towards our final experience of the 'good'.

There is a realism expressed here that Generation Y can appreciate. Young people are not looking for Christian leaders to provide trite answers that explain away the pain or excuse God in the light of suffering. Young people are looking for a realism that grapples with the reality of suffering, so we do them a disservice by providing simplistic answers to complex issues. We will never be able to encourage deep discipleship if we take that approach. Discipling Generation Y will inevitably involve confessing our own ignorance in the face of the big questions of life just as much as it will involve sharing the wisdom of our experience. Perhaps a realisation of our ignorance is the greatest wisdom that our experience has left us with. In 1 Corinthians 13:12, Paul says, 'At the present time, we see through a mirror obscurely.'* We must not be ashamed to stand with Paul in that statement. Young people will appreciate our honesty and will respond positively.

Generation Y Christians will interpret the signs of the times. They will read their own pain, they will read the suffering of the world, and they will come to their own conclusions. The message of John's Revelation is clear: our task is to help them interpret the pain within the broader narrative of God's sovereignty and final victory. The good news is that God's victory becomes our own through our union with the resurrected and ascended Christ (Romans 6:4–5). As Jesus said to the Christians at Philadelphia: 'Because you have kept my word of patient endurance, I will keep you from the hour of trial that is coming on the whole world to test the inhabitants of the earth. I am coming soon; hold fast to what you have, so that no one may seize your crown' (Revelation 3:10–11).

As we minister to Generation Y believers, we do not want to disciple them into passivity but into an active engagement with the mission of the church in the light of what they see and experience. As they perceive the signs, persevere in their pain and pray for the world, so they will grow in the image and likeness of Christ. Out of that will develop a desire to engage proactively in matters of social justice, for the glory of God, which is the topic of our next chapter.

Some questions to consider

- What do you think of the idea that God can use suffering and chaos to bring about warnings and judgment on humanity?

- Is it necessary to believe in a literal fall of Adam and Eve to have a concept of a fallen and disordered creation?
- What examples from around the world can you think of where God may have used a catastrophe to bring a judgment or a warning?
- How can you communicate this theology to your young people without encouraging them to see all suffering as a judgment of God on individual people?
- How might you encourage your young people into a discipleship pattern that takes seriously perseverance and prayer?
- What does it mean for you personally to persevere in the faith?

Chapter 6

What can I do about social injustice?

Generation Y: concern for the world

It was the Labour MP Tony Benn who said that he was leaving
Parliament so that he could get back to being involved in politics.
It was a courageous statement that accorded perfectly with the
mindset of 21st-century Britain. It appears that the days of sustained institutional mass membership are well and truly over.
Fewer people are joining political parties, fewer people are joining
societal institutions and fewer people are joining the church. The
reasons for this are many and varied, of course, but at the heart of
this move away from institutional alignment, as Tony Benn rightly
observed, is a belief that change comes less through the activity of
cumbersome organisations (whether political or faith-based) and
more through localised and targeted engagement. If we want to
make a difference in the world, we will not do it through joining
a political party. We will do it through micro-engagement on a
community level.

That type of thinking is a sign of the times. You may remember
the 2011 riots that started in London and then engulfed many
major cities and towns in the UK. Truly terrible scenes of looting,
arson and mob violence filled our screens, culminating in the sad
demise of major landmarks and businesses and in the deaths of
five people. In the immediate aftermath, however, a great many

good people took to the streets with their brooms and cleaned up the devastation. They were not responding to a political initiative; they were answering a call for micro-engagement that grew out of a Twitter campaign. There is a growing awareness of the power of micro-engagement and a number of networks are developing to aid the cause. For example, the 38 Degrees network (so called because this is the critical angle at which an avalanche may commence) brings together people to take action on local causes. At the time of writing, there are 3.8 million people active in the network— more people than in all the major political parties of Britain added together. By the time you read this, there will undoubtedly be many more.

Despite many people's criticism, the truth is that Generation Y is an engaged generation. Young people today are concerned about social injustice. They despise war and poverty. They are far less discriminatory and far more accepting than previous genera-tions. Young people want to see the eradication of inequality and marginalisation. However, unlike their predecessors, they do not believe in the power of the institution to bring about radical and permanent change. They are distrustful of the machinery of society, considering those in power to be greedy and self-seeking. Quite rightly, their desire for social improvement is tempered with a deep cynicism about the desire of those from previous generations to work for the same ends. Generation Y wants to change the world but does not want to pay membership subs to do it.

The impact of this culture for the church is huge. It is rare to see a young person tithe their pocket money or hard-earned Saturday job wage into the collection plate. Why would they want to hand money over to be used for the perpetuation of an institution that they do not really believe in? But this does not mean that Generation Y is ungenerous. Instead, they will use their money in a different way to make a point. For those of us working with young people, it is far easier to engage them through Slum Survivor, the sponsorship of a child in the global South, or by providing products for a foodbank than it is to encourage a regular, weekly pattern of financial giving.

While we are pleased to encourage young people in micro-engagement, we must not be naïve about the long-term impact of this strategy of discipling. Currently, it is the Silent Generation and Baby Boomers who financially uphold the church. In 20 years' time, when their giving has decreased dramatically either through death or incapacity, the financial gap will not be filled by Generation X or Generation Y. This will have a seismic impact on how we do church: buildings, salaried workers, centralised mission, marketing and resourcing will all be under threat or severely rationalised. It will not mark the demise of the kingdom work of the church, but it will mean a radical overhaul of values and how the church is structured for mission.

In essence, Generation Y is concerned to engage in real-time prophetic activity. Generation Y sees the need and wants to meet the need, not form a sub-committee to talk about the problem. Advances in social media networking are facilitating this approach to politicised engagement at an almost frightening rate. If the church is to be successful in discipling Generation Y, it must be willing to reassess its use of social media and its own vision, to work at the level of effective micro-engagement rather than corporate strategic missional activity. In the light of John's vision in Revelation, there are three areas in particular that must be at the heart of our discipling activity with Generation Y—political oppression, religious oppression and the reality of structural sin.

Combating political oppression

Given the cultural milieu in which John was writing, it is not surprising to discover that the issue of political oppression infuses Revelation. Such antagonism had been the backdrop of Christian experience from the very beginning. Even as a baby or young child, Jesus himself had been carried to Egypt for fear of the retribution of

Herod (Matthew 2:14). The Romans had crucified him and pursued Paul and the other disciples to death. Nero had persecuted and blamed the Christians for all manner of ills, not least the burning of Rome. As we have noted, political oppression was predominantly economic rather than physical under Domitian, but the pain was still intense. John was writing to Christians in Asia Minor who were living in fear for their security and lives. The first hearers and readers of the vision were trying to make sense of their faith in the light of this oppression, and John addresses their concern through profoundly symbolic language, not least in chapter 13.

In 13:1, John tells us, 'I saw a beast rising out of the sea.' We have already considered how the sea is a biblical metaphor for chaos, but the sea is also the route by which the troops of the Roman Empire would have come to Asia Minor. The persecuting powers that appeared on the horizon would surely have looked like a beast coming out of the sea. John describes the beast as having 'on its horns... ten diadems, and on its heads... blasphemous names'. This multitude of heads and horns suggests almost an exact replica of the dragon in Revelation 12, so John is telling us that this beast is very much in the image and under the control of Satan. There is, however, one interesting difference. In 12:3, the dragon had 'seven diadems on his heads', but in 13:1, the beast has ten diadems on his horns. Since 'horns' symbolise aggression in Revelation, we can infer that oppressive political regimes hold on to power through violence.

The rest of the description in 13:2 is an amalgamation of the beasts seen by Daniel in his vision, recorded in Daniel 7. For this Old Testament prophet, they represented four oppressive foreign powers—Babylon, Media, Persia and Greece. John combines them all in his vision to make the point that the beast from the sea represents all oppressive regimes throughout history. The blasphemous names on its heads indicate that they stand in opposition to God. The seeming invincibility of oppressive political regimes is indicated in 13:3, where John states, 'One of its heads seemed to have received a death-blow, but its mortal wound had been healed. In amazement the whole earth followed the beast.' History clearly shows us that political oppression is resurrected time and time again. Just when we think that an oppressive regime is mortally wounded, it revives and grows strong again. It is the seeming invincibility of the political power that leaves people in amazement.

John engages in a game of parody in Revelation 13 and 19, comparing the false claims of the beast with the true claims of Christ. If the dragon wants to be God, then the beast is its Christ-figure. The beast has ten diadems and, in 19:12, we are told Christ has many diadems. The beast has a blasphemous name but, in 19:16, the name inscribed on Christ's thigh denotes him as worthy of our praise: 'King of kings and Lord of lords'. The beast causes people to worship the dragon but Christ causes us to worship the Father. The beast has a wound but lives, and Christ too was wounded but lives. The beast is given authority by the dragon and Christ is given authority by the Father. So the exclamation in 13:4, 'Who is like the beast, and who can fight against it?' reminds us of Exodus 15:11, where Israel proclaims, 'Who is like you, O Lord, among the gods?' It's not surprising, then, that in Revelation 13:5 'The beast was given a mouth uttering haughty and blasphemous words.'

The nature of the blasphemy in 13:6 is very interesting: 'It opened its mouth to utter blasphemies against God, blaspheming his name and his dwelling, that is, those who dwell in heaven.' This verse gives us great encouragement when we remember that *we* are God's dwelling. When we are reviled for the faith or suffer persecution, God dwells within us by his Holy Spirit and gives us the strength to endure. Sadly, John moves into the future tense in verse 8 when he comments, 'And all the inhabitants of the earth will worship it.' He is telling us that, until the end comes, there will always be oppressors leading political regimes that will persecute God's people, supported by those whose names are not written in the book of life.

Combating religious oppression

Just as the early history of the church was written in the blood of political oppression and martyrdom, so was it written in the language of terror caused by religious oppression. Jesus had been maligned by the Pharisees and the Sadducees, the religious leaders of the day conspiring with the political authorities to have him crucified, and the first disciples had endured an uneasy relationship with the synagogue. The letters to the seven churches in Revelation 2—3 clearly reveal the antipathy of many Jewish communities towards this new movement called 'the Way' or, later, 'Christianity'. Through Revelation, John exposed religious oppression for what it truly was.

The second beast described by John in chapter 13 arises not from the sea but from the earth. In verse 11, John says that 'it had two horns like a lamb and it spoke like a dragon'. This seems to be more innocuous than the first beast: after all, it is described as being like a lamb, with the same word, *arnion*, that was used for Christ as the Lamb in 5:6. For all its religiosity and meekness, however, this second beast speaks like a dragon. In 13:12, we see the religiosity and the evil of the beast come together: 'It exercises all the authority of the first beast on its behalf, and it makes the earth and its inhabitants worship the first beast, whose mortal wound had been healed.' It is clear that this beast is the cult of emperor worship: remember that Domitian carried the title 'Lord and God' and Roman citizens worshipped him as an incarnation of god. But what has this to say to us today, as we have no Roman emperor to worship?

John is drawing our attention to the way in which oppressive regimes often support their ideologies through religious beliefs and, conversely, how some expressions of faith actively support political authority as the outworking of God's will in the secular realm. We remember the link between the Nazis and the Lutheran Church in the 1930s, each justifying the actions of the other, working together in anti-Semitism. We remember the South African apartheid movement that claimed Christianity as its basis for belief. We think, most obviously today, of Islamists who justify their terrorism by faith. We might also reflect on how fundamentalist Christianity in the United States shows support for right-wing politicians as if their policies were the outworking of Christian faith, and we could be critical of politicians in Britain who have used Christianity as a means of justifying particular policy decisions. The first beast and the second beast work hand in hand.

The second beast engages in great spiritual activities to win respect for itself: for example, 'It performs great signs, even making fire come down from heaven to earth in the sight of all' (13:13). Again, we are reminded of Jesus' prophecy in Mark 13:22 that 'false Christs and false prophets will appear and perform signs and miracles to deceive the elect' (NIV). Of course, the idea of prophets calling down fire from heaven reminds us of the story about Elijah and the prophets of Ba'al in 1 Kings 18:38. However, the ultimate blasphemy is recorded in Revelation 13:15: 'and it was allowed to give breath to the image of the beast'. In Genesis 2:7, it is God who gives the breath of life, so for the beast to seek to usurp that gift is the most disgusting idolatry possible.

Combating structural sin

Underpinning both political and religious oppression is the notion of structural sin. It is in Revelation 17 that John gives his clearest exposition of God's judgment on this reality. Here we discover God's anger, expressed with alarming frankness, towards the structures of civilisation that oppress and marginalise those who are unable to secure their own rights. We see condemned before God the political and economic structures that favour the rich at the expense of the poor. As a result of Revelation 17, we are forced to consider afresh our interaction with these structures.

The harsh reality is in evidence at the very beginning, with the opening words of the angel to John in verse 1: 'Come, I will show you the judgment of the great whore who is seated on many waters.' The woman on this beast is a metaphor for civilised society that stands in organised opposition to God. It is important to note that she is called a prostitute rather than an adulterer. In the Old Testament, Israel was accused by the Lord of committing adultery against him by chasing after false gods. That is the primary motif for Hosea's life but it is also a theme in the writings of the major prophets. John's reference to the woman in Revelation 17 as a prostitute rather than an adulterer prevents any possible confusion of identity. In Isaiah 23:16–17 and Nahum 3, those described as prostitutes were nation states and cities that stood accused before God for their insolent and rebellious ways. The fact that the woman sits on 'many waters' is significant as a reference to the nations' ungodliness being worked out predominantly through commerce, business and trade. Business took place across the Middle East through its intricate network of waterways. In Jeremiah 51:13, Babylon is addressed as 'you opulent city, standing beside great waters', and Psalm 137 begins, 'By the rivers of Babylon, we sat and wept' (NIV). The disgusting immorality of economic and national greed through commerce is underlined in Revelation 17:2: 'with whom the kings of the earth have committed fornication, and with the wine of whose fornication the inhabitants of the earth have become drunk'. Political leaders join in the sins of the prostitute. The fornication of economists does not remain isolated to them alone: political leaders and the inhabitants of the earth have all become drunk on the wine of their fornication.

A fresh perspective on the prostitute is given in 17:3, where she is shown riding on the back of the beast. Given what we have considered above, we recognise that structural sin rides on the back of oppressive political and religious power. More correctly, since 'the beast' is a central figure in Revelation, oppressive political and religious regimes give support to ungodly structures in society. In verse 4, the woman is described in more detail: she 'was clothed in purple and scarlet, and adorned with gold and jewels and pearls, holding in her hand a golden cup full of abominations and the impurities of her fornication'. The opulence and luxury of the woman's appearance are lurid and exaggerated. Scarlet is indicative of great wealth, while purple was extracted from a rare shellfish called murex. Like some object of ultimate luxury, she is covered in gold and jewels and pearls. She holds in her hand a golden cup that we would expect to contain something beautiful but it is full of abominations and filth. In Jeremiah 51:7, God says, 'Babylon was a golden cup... making all the earth drunken; the nations drank of her wine, and so the nations went mad.' A golden cup, signifying regal glory, contains the filth of abomination. Such is the state of the fallen world in which we find ourselves.

The result of the flow of her ungodliness is quite shocking: 'And I saw that the woman was drunk with the blood of the saints and the blood of the witnesses to Jesus' (17:6). There is something quite horrific about this image because it suggests that those who are antichrist take perverse delight in the suffering of the people of God and the humiliation of the church. That is not to say, of course, that all people delight in the physical torture and murder of Christians, but we know from recent times that great delight is taken by many when the church is pilloried in the media over its falling numbers or its stance on ethical issues.

Preaching an unwelcome message

When we consider the cumulative power of political oppression, religious oppression and structural sin, we are left aghast, wondering what sort of response to make. For the purposes of this book, we wonder how best to disciple Generation Y so that they may challenge social injustice where it becomes evident, for it is clear that Generation Y must be discipled to unmask and challenge the evils of ungodly society. There is culpability in silence: if we are not part of the solution, we are part of the problem. It is not good discipleship to stand idly by while society tolerates injustice and the continuing marginalisation of the poor, the weak and the vulnerable. We must teach young people to speak up for truth and for what is right. Speaking into the silence diminishes the power of evil—that much is certain—but we must be honest with our young people and tell them that such a stance will involve preaching a most unwelcome message. It is clear from Revelation 11:1–13 that the church in the last days will face persecution as it carries out its responsibilities for mission. John is specific about the fact that not every Christian will be persecuted; nevertheless, persecution will become a more normative feature for Generation Y.

In 11:1–2, John is told to measure the people of God, symbolised by the temple in accordance with Paul's understanding (1 Corinthians 3:16; 2 Corinthians 6:16; Ephesians 2:21). The act of measuring symbolises God's protection of his people, not as a promise to save us from persecution but as a promise that the church will not be entirely lost to persecution. Those who stand firm in the face of persecution are described in 11:3 as the 'two witnesses'. They will be dressed in sackcloth as a symbol of mourning, since the prophetic role of Generation Y Christians will be, in no small part, to mourn the godlessness of society.

Mixing his metaphors somewhat in verse 4, John now portrays the two witnesses as two olive trees and two lampstands—ideas that are drawn from Zechariah 4. This should be a real encouragement for young people as we disciple them into the rigour of mission because there is a link between olive oil and the Holy Spirit, and between a lampstand and the presence of Christ. Generation Y may be called to proclaim the gospel in an inhospitable environment where they face ridicule and persecution but they go in the strength, power and presence of Christ and the Holy Spirit. Nevertheless, verse 7 gives serious pause for thought. 'When they have finished their testimony, the beast that comes up from the bottomless pit will make war on them and conquer them and kill them.' This is a hard verse for us to comprehend because it tells us that God has set a period of time for the witnesses to testify and then, when their testimony is over, they will be killed. As hard as it is for us to stomach this idea, it is the harsh reality for the persecuted church. The beast of political oppression that comes up from the bottomless pit does indeed conquer and kill Christians. We are given a stark reminder that some Christians will pay the ultimate price for their faith at the hands of evil political regimes and that they will be treated with shameful disdain: 'and their dead bodies will lie in the street of the great city that is prophetically called Sodom and Egypt, where also their Lord was crucified' (v. 8). Wherever wickedness and oppression happen, there the Lord is crucified. So, rather than thinking of this 'great city' as Jerusalem, we should see it as a metaphorical reference to all cities where Christ is opposed in word and deed. It is there that the faithful proclaimers of the gospel are killed, treated with disdain and made a laughing stock, as their bodies are, metaphorically, left to rot in public view.

Verse 11, however, begins with this promise: 'But after the three and a half days, the breath of life from God entered them, and they stood on their feet, and those who saw them were terrified.' What vindication! What triumph for the Church of God! As Paul says in Romans 8:35-37, 'What can separate us from the love of Christ? Can affliction, or hardship? Can persecution, hunger, nakedness, danger or sword? … We have been treated like sheep for slaughter and yet, through it all, we are more than conquerors through him who loves us.'* The Church may be persecuted to the point of extinction, the world may gloat, the world may treat us with disdain, and our corporate body may be fed to the dogs and covered with shame, but resurrection is ours in Jesus Christ. The Church of Christ shall never be overcome and the people shall be terrified because the Spirit of God—the reviving, resurrecting Spirit—is at work within us. That is good news indeed!

Responding to social injustice

Generation Y Christians have an enormous burden of mission awaiting them. We do them a disservice if we do not alert them to the seriousness of that mission and the inherent dangers of engaging with it. We must be truthful as we disciple our young people. However, we can assure them that, as they undertake the task of mission in the 21st century, they go in the authority of God, in the power of the Spirit and carrying the light of Christ. They may have to endure political oppression; they may be treated with disdain and covered in shame; the world may rejoice at their failures, but ultimately they will be raised and taken up to heaven with God.

At the heart of Generation Y missionary activity will be the need to challenge political and religious regimes that marginalise and oppress those without a voice in society. Generation Y Christians will need to have a prophetic ministry in naming the powers that oppress and support oppression. Of course, metaphorically speaking, they will want to address the prostitute of Revelation 17 by dealing with the symptoms of oppression—homelessness, racism, civil war, torture and so on—but the prophetic and missional calling of Generation Y, ultimately, is to name the beast, to unveil the beast and let people see it for what it really is. A ministry of social awareness is not limited to dealing with the problems but is fundamentally about naming the powers of evil that run through the DNA of so many of our institutions, whether they are political, religious or economic.

Christ came to this broken world and gave himself sacrificially for it. Generation Y Christians are being called to follow that example by living sacrificial lives as they seek to meet the needs of suffering and vulnerable people. A Generation Y church must rediscover a hunger and passion for the pursuit of social justice. It must speak out against unjust wars; it must seek to be a reconciling presence in the midst of civil disorder; it must stand for ecological justice and turn its practices towards the re-greening of the earth. A Generation Y church must do more than throw a few quid towards the starving; it must challenge the institutions perpetuating a world order that not only tolerates the existence of famine but actually creates it. Those of us who are involved in discipling Generation Y must think carefully about how we might facilitate this ministry.

Some questions to consider

- In what ways is your local church engaged in addressing issues of social injustice, either locally or globally? To what extent are the young people you work with engaged in that agenda?
- What are the social injustice concerns of your young people? How might you creatively encourage them to address those issues and make a real difference?
- To what extent do we teach 'safe' discipleship to the young people we work with? What might be the response if we taught them about the possibility of persecution and hardship as a result of their future missional activity?
- How can your young people develop a prophetic ministry to your local church with regard to engagement with social injustice?
- How might you 'politicise' your young people more?
- Do you need to become more politicised yourself? How might you address that need?

Chapter 7

What is the final judgment of God?

Generation Y: guilt, shame and sin

When it comes to discipling Generation Y, it is very hard indeed to nurture a belief in God's final judgment. This is for four primary reasons.

First, communication of the doctrine of final judgment has historically been bound in with current culture. However, the willingness of the church to adapt its picture of that event has not kept pace with the speed of cultural change, resulting in a credibility gap between the doctrine and the perception of young people. For many years, the image of the final judgment was one of people queuing up before a throne while an angel read from a huge ledger. Depending on what was in the ledger, the deceased human would then be directed right to glory or left to damnation. With advances in technology in the 1980s, the symbolism shifted, so that we imagined our sins being played out before us on a huge video screen in heaven. However useful these images may or may not have been, they are certainly bound to a particular culture. We are unable to do justice to a doctrine if we present it to Generation Y in the cultural format of previous generations. The doctrine itself appears implausible because the medium by which it is delivered seems outmoded and irrelevant.

Second, the notion of final judgment is inextricably bound up with a metanarrative that does not sit easily with Generation Y. The very idea that individual acts can have such serious eternal consequences is not part of the worldview of a generation that lives in moments of immediacy. That form of understanding demands a linear story, with a beginning and an end, and the idea of personal guilt needs to be located within the unfolding of that story. But the postmodern condition is one in which the notion of the story itself has come under scrutiny. If the story is not to be trusted, then there is no place for the type of guilt that results in final judgment. That is not to say that young people do not feel guilt and shame— such emotions are common to the human condition—but their guilt and shame are more localised than eternal. Young people will feel guilt and shame over the way in which they have treated a friend or a friendship group but, once the issue has been sorted out, the guilt dissipates and life returns to normal.

This relates to the third difficulty, which is a generational difference in naming the actuality of sin. Many patterns of behaviour that were labelled 'sinful' by previous generations are now either fully acceptable to Generation Y or are deemed to be 'lifestyle choices' rather than 'sin'. Homosexual relationships, sex before marriage, indulging in soft drugs, binge drinking, living beyond financial means and so on are no longer abhorrent practices to this liberalised generation. While many young people will deem some of this behaviour as not advantageous, they would not want to deny others the right to indulge if they so wish. Generation Y is socially liberal yet relationally conservative in its understanding of behavioural acceptability. This has an impact on the way in which the church's teaching on sin and judgment is heard.

Fourth, we must acknowledge the embarrassment factor that many Christian youth workers feel in talking to young people about the idea of final judgment. For one thing, the stark reality is that youth workers are so pleased to have young people enquire about the faith that they do not want to put them off by talk of sin and judgment. Verging on modern-day Marcionism, much youth work practice focuses almost exclusively on the 'God of love' revealed in the ministry of Jesus Christ and seeks to avoid the 'angry God' who is mistakenly assumed to predominate in the Old Testament and makes a return on Judgment Day. This approach to discipling is born out of a fear that too much talk of sin and judgment will result in the loss of young people to the faith. How much easier it is to speak of mercy, forgiveness and love than anger, wrath and judgment.

The embarrassment factor is also a result of confused doctrinal understanding about the nature of Christ. I have argued elsewhere, in my book *Models for Youth Ministry*, that youth workers often teach erroneous Christology by speaking of the Christ who is still present with us, living in our hearts. This is not true: Jesus has ascended to heaven; he is gone. Certainly, God is still present to us—but through his Holy Spirit, not Jesus Christ. If we do not teach the doctrine of an absent Christ, we are unable to teach the doctrine of the second coming and then we have no basis for expounding the final judgment. Quite simply, youth workers are forced into an embarrassing corner, unable to teach about the final judgment with integrity, because they have not constructed a theological system that can find a natural place for this doctrine. When youth workers take seriously the ascension of Christ and its implications for pastoral ministry, then teaching about the final judgment will become more natural.

The ideas of ongoing judgment and a final judgment are inter-woven throughout John's Revelation. For him, they are an integral part of the story and enable believers to make sense of their current predicament. If we are to help young people make sense of their life experiences and make rational decisions about their life choices, we must help them locate the immediacy of the moment within a metanarrative that takes judgment seriously. To do that, we must develop a better understanding of the reasons for judgment, what is being and to be judged, and a more nuanced understanding about what Revelation says and does not say about the final judgment itself.

The reason for God's judgment

Before we consider God's judgment in detail, it is fair to ask the question, 'Why does he need to judge anyway?' Although John does not give a comprehensive answer to this in Revelation (his teaching must be supplemented by that of other biblical writers), we are given an insight through 6:9–10: 'I saw under the altar the souls of those who had been slain because of the word of God and the testimony they had maintained. They called out in a loud voice, "How long, Sovereign Lord, holy and true, until you judge the inhabitants of the earth and avenge our blood?"' (NIV).

We must go back to the beginning of scripture to trace the origin of this idea. It is in Genesis 4:10 that we first encounter the idea of the souls of the righteous crying out to God. After Cain had slain Abel, God came to him and enquired, 'What have you done? Listen! Your brother's blood cries out to me from the ground' (NIV). This is a really evocative picture from the first book of the Bible, matched by a similarly evocative picture from 6:9–10 in the last book of the Bible, where the saints are crying out to God again, asking when their spilt blood will be avenged. Matthew 23:35 provides a parallel through Jesus' warning to the Pharisees in which he says, 'Upon you will come all the righteous blood that has been shed on earth, from the blood of righteous Abel to the blood of Zechariah son of Berekiah, whom you murdered between the temple and the altar' (NIV). Clearly, God will judge the world for the way in which it has slain his martyrs.

In Revelation 6:9, the souls of the martyrs are pictured as being 'under the altar'. There are two ideas coming together here. The first is from Leviticus 4:7, where instructions are given about sacrificing animals on the altar: 'The priest shall then put some of the blood on the horns of the altar of fragrant incense that is before the Lord in the Tent of Meeting. The rest of the bull's blood he shall pour out at the base of the altar' (NIV). There is also a Jewish text by Rabbi Akiba that speaks of being buried under the altar in the temple as a symbol of resting for all eternity under the glory and power of God. It is therefore interesting that the Greek word used in verse 10 for 'Lord' is not the one usually used of Jesus, as in 'Lord Jesus'. Normally, we would expect to find the word *kyrios*, but the word used is *despotes*, from which we derive the word 'despot'. There is an indication here of absolute authority and power in God as he comes to judge the world for the deaths of the martyrs.

We may think that the prayer of the martyrs is a little selfish; the avenging of their blood seems a strangely self-centred request. However, what they are asking for is the vindication of truth and holiness, not revenge for their early deaths. The fact that they address God as 'Sovereign Lord, holy and true' is a clear indication of that priority. They know that truth and holiness will be finally vindicated only when Christ returns again, so theirs is a call for the second coming, when God will be finally glorified throughout the whole of creation. That second coming will inevitably be accompanied by the final judgment, so, in conclusion, we realise that the need for God to judge is inextricably bound up with the revelation of his glory, righteousness and power. We simply cannot have one without the other.

Judgment on civilisation

The final judgment is most fully detailed in Revelation 14 and 20, but we must first give some detailed consideration to Revelation 18 as a precursor to that event. This passage speaks of destruction on a mass scale, the annihilation of all civilised society. We reflected on God's anger at the oppressive structures of society when we considered the prostitute, named in 17:5 as Babylon the Great. Chapter 18 concerns the fall and destruction of Babylon, metaphorically representing civilisation without God, which operates through oppressive politics, oppressive business practices and oppressive economics. Its absolute destruction is the precursor to the final judgment.

Revelation 18 portrays the end of the world as we know it, as a result of God's judgment. Previously, John outlined God's judgments and warnings through the metaphors of seals, trumpets and bowls of wrath, but now he goes further, describing the death of civilisation in horrifying detail. In doing so, he draws together imagery from a number of Old Testament passages in which nation states and cities that stand in opposition to God come under judgment (for example, the destruction of Babylon in Isaiah 13 and Jeremiah 51, the destruction of Tyre in Ezekiel 26, the prophecies against Edom in Isaiah 34 and the prophecy against Nineveh in Nahum 3). Babylon, a wondrous city in the Middle East with a rich history, is now described in horrendous terms: 'It has become a dwelling-place of demons... a haunt of every foul bird, a haunt of every foul and hateful beast' (Revelation 18:2). In verse 3, John specifically names civilised society, oppressive political rulers and those engaged in oppressive business practice as being responsible for the downfall of human civilisation. The whole earth, it seems, has become corrupted by idolatry, persecution and greed.

There is a temptation for us all to make peace with Babylon, and these temptations are greater still for Generation Y. It has become easy for young people to get drunk on wine, enjoy low interest rates, indulge in hedonistic practices and purchase cheap goods that have been produced on the backs of the exploited poor, but this passage is a stark reminder that there is a spiritual issue at stake in the way we engage with the world. Jesus' words recorded in John 17:14–15 suggest that, as his followers, we do not belong to the world even though this is our current abode. Likewise, Peter reminded his readers that they were 'aliens and exiles' and should 'abstain from the desires of the flesh that wage war against the soul' (1 Peter 2:11). As Christians, we must be mindful of how we live out our lives. There is a fine line between engaging in responsible societal activity and getting drunk on the wine of Babylon, and the line is not always clear for us to see. In the passion and energy of youth, it is even harder for young people. Part of our task in discipling

Generation Y is to help them heed the cry of 18:4: 'Come out of her, my people, so that you do not take part in her sins, and so that you do not share in her plagues.' We must educate young people in the urgency of their situation. If they get metaphorically drunk on the wine of Babylon, if they become consumed with materialism or careless in their ethical practices, they are playing with fire—the fire of God's judgment. In his justice, God cannot overlook or ignore the sins of civilised society. As verse 5 reminds us so graphically, 'her sins are heaped as high as heaven'. The Greek word translated 'heaped' is *kollao*, which suggests that the sins of the earth are glued together, inextricably linked in a pile that reaches to heaven. They are in the line of God's eyesight, so he cannot possibly ignore them. John reminds us, 'God has remembered her iniquities' (v. 5).

The mechanics of God's judgment upon ungodly civilisation are skilfully introduced in verse 6: 'Render to her as she herself has rendered, and repay her double for her deeds; mix a double draught for her in the cup she mixed.' If this command were being given to the people of God, it would be difficult to comprehend. It would give permission for Christians to engage in wholesale slaughter and vindictive retribution. Not only would we repay Babylon for her evils; we would dish out a double portion of retribution. But that reading does not accord with John's intent in Revelation. At no point do we encounter the idea that it is the role of Christians to act as ministers of God's judgment. In fact, the very opposite is true. John more often calls us to passive resistance, allowing God to do the judging. We must not read 18:6 in a sense of 'holy war'—engaging in acts of slaughter and retribution in the name of God. Instead, the ministers of God's judgment have consistently been shown to be those who themselves are to be judged. Throughout Revelation, it is clearly shown that the powers of evil turn in on themselves, that there is no unity in antichrist. Demons fight demons, oppressive kings fight oppressive kings and sin rises up in sin against sin. The consequence of fallen civilisation is that it will turn in upon itself and will mete out violence and revenge from within its own ranks. The end of civilisation will come about through internal fragmentation as evil declares civil war upon itself. That is how God's judgment will be realised.

Many would argue that this is what is happening in the present age. Economic structures are imploding, nation states descending into civil war and sectarian ideologies squaring up against each other, to their own detriment. The narrative of the world's ills does seem to be an implosion as evil fights against itself and seeks revenge against itself. The irony is that civilisation does not seem to recognise this process in action, as John prophesies in 18:7: 'She glorified herself and lived luxuriously... Since in her heart she says, "I rule as a queen; I am no widow, and I will never see grief."' This is self-delusion in the extreme. God's judgment is coming and it will be swift in its delivery, as promised in verse 8: 'Therefore her plagues will come in a single day.' As we seek to disciple Generation Y, we want to encourage young people to read the signs of the times so that they can make appropriate life choices as well as speaking prophetically into their own context and friendship groups.

As we considered in the last chapter, the prophetic message that our young people are to proclaim will not be popular—it is stark and harsh—but it must be spoken into the ills of our current society. In Revelation 18, we gain three further insights into the detail of what Generation Y believers must proclaim.

First, they must unmask the lack of integrity inherent within structurally sinful institutions. Ultimately, there is no loyalty to be found within oppressive organisations. It is a crucial observation that those who mourn the passing of civilisation in Revelation 18— the kings, the merchants and the shipmasters—all do so as they 'stand far off' (vv. 10, 15, 17). As civilisation collapses, they all escape and mourn from a distance. None of them are prepared to stay on the Titanic as it sinks. Ultimately, they are cowards and egocentric grabbers of power and wealth. When the city starts to collapse, they are the first to get out. Furthermore, they do not mourn the loss of Babylon so much as the loss of their personal gains, power and prestige. In verse 9, the kings weep and wail because they 'lived in luxury with her'. In verse 11, the merchants weep and mourn because 'no one buys their cargo any more'. In verse 19, the shipmasters weep and mourn as they remember the fact that 'all who had ships at sea grew rich by her wealth'. Part of the prophetic task before Generation Y believers is to unmask the selfishness of structurally sinful institutions.

Second, Generation Y believers must be encouraged to unmask the human misery behind exploitative business practices. In Revelation 18:12–13, John lists the cargo that made the merchants rich. Fifteen products are mentioned in this list, the last of them being 'human lives'. Given the cultural context of Revelation, this is not so much a condemnation of the slave trade (although we might infer that) as a comment on how immoral business practices and banking practices have a negative impact on ordinary people. Those who sell goods produced in sweatshops are condemned here, alongside the employers who have not given a fair wage for a fair day's work, the employers who have exploited, manipulated and threatened their workers, and so on. There is a human cost behind every exploitative business practice. A prophetic ministry must expose this evil for what it is.

Third, Generation Y believers must convince their peers of the impermanence of civilisation. In 18:21 we read, 'Then a mighty angel took up a stone like a great millstone and threw it into the sea, saying, "With such violence Babylon the great city will be thrown down, and will be found no more."' We are reminded of Jeremiah 51:64, where the prophet commands that the scroll of his prophecies should be tied to a stone and thrown into the River Euphrates, with the words, 'Thus shall Babylon sink, to rise no more.' The finality of God's judgment is quite terrifying:

The sound of harpists and minstrels and of flautists and trumpeters will be heard in you no more; and an artisan of any trade will be found in you no more; and the sound of the millstone will be heard in you no more; and the light of a lamp will shine in you no more; and the voice of bridegroom and bride will be heard in you no more. (Revelation 18:22–23)

All is lost. Civilisation will be judged and will be no more. Young Christians must do what they can to help others see this impermanence and help them to seek the permanent. At the heart of the Generation Y mission imperative is this advice from Jesus, recorded in Matthew 6:19–21:

'Do not store up for yourselves treasures on earth, where moth and rust consume and where thieves break in and steal; but store up for yourselves treasures in heaven, where neither moth nor rust consumes and where thieves do not break in and steal. For where your treasure is, there your heart will be also.'

The final judgment

The final judgment that follows the annihilation of human society is completely different from anything that has come before. Until this point, God has given warnings and judgments within the course of human history, metaphorically represented through seals, trumpets and bowls of wrath, but the final judgment is performed outside of time.

As we disciple Generation Y, we must teach them the reality of final judgment, but not through speculative theology. John does not give details about God's methodology. Instead, he focuses on the theological implications of judgment for us. We must dissuade young people from pursuing a thirst for detail that is not biblical. The nature and methodology of judgment are not for us to know. Our concern is only that it will happen and that we must respond with missionary zeal and intent.

The angel mentioned in 14:15 calls out to God, 'Use your sickle and reap, for the hour to reap has come, because the harvest of the earth is fully ripe.' In John's Gospel, as well as in Revelation, the phrase 'the hour' is a significant one. At the wedding in Cana, Jesus says, 'My hour has not yet come' (John 2:4). In 12:23, he says, 'The hour has come for the Son of Man to be glorified' and again in verse 27, 'It is for this reason that I have come to this hour.' In 17:1, he prays, 'Father, the hour has come.' For John, 'the hour' speaks of the inevitability of things coming to their climax. At the final judgment, the hour has come to reap and harvest the earth. The fact that 'the harvest of the earth is fully ripe' indicates that there is nothing arbitrary about the Day of Judgment. Even though we may question why God delays, his timing is perfect and we must trust in that.

Although Revelation 14:14–20 does not give any real details of God's methodology for final judgment, we are given an insight into the passion of the event. In verse 19, we read that the angel swung his sickle to reap the harvest and 'threw it into the great wine press of the wrath of God'. The wrath (or anger) of God has already been mentioned twice in chapter 14, specifically in verse 10: 'They will also drink the wine of God's wrath, poured unmixed into the cup of his anger.' However, it is significant that John uses two different Greek words here for 'anger' and 'wrath'. 'The wine of God's wrath' is described by the word *thumos*, which is the type of wrath driven by passion and emotion, while, in describing 'the cup of his anger', John uses the word *orge*, which is less emotion-driven and more to do with righteous indignation. When the final judgment is described in verse 19, John again uses the word *thumos*. For God, the final judgment is a passionate, emotional response that seeks an end to the horror of sin. John presents a deeply emotional and evocative picture here.

The moment of judgment is described in 20:11–15 but, again, not in any great detail. The methodology is not as important as the implications. In verse 11, John states, 'I saw a great white throne and the one seated upon it, from before whom the earth and the heaven fled, and a place was not found for them.'* At the heart of the final judgment is the immense glory of God. The gravitas of what is to come is emphasised by heaven and earth fleeing away. At this moment, the judgment throne of God is the only reality in the universe; nothing else matters. John records in verse 12, 'I saw the dead, great and small, standing before the throne, and books were opened. Also another book was opened, the book of life. And the dead were judged according to their works, as recorded in the books.' As we seek to disciple young people into a better understanding of the final judgment, we must note two things from this verse. First, the whole of humanity stands before God in judgment. There is no room for the erroneous belief that Christians somehow bypass judgment. That is plainly not true. Everyone is judged, both great and small. Second, the phrase 'judged according to their works' does not suggest that salvation comes through doing good deeds. (If the book of life were not mentioned too—the book in whose names are written Christ's elect—then that may be the case.) But it does indicate that we are involved in writing our own destiny. Our deeds are good indicators as to the nature of our commitment to Christ. They indicate the nature of our relationship with Jesus, by which we are judged. In the appearance of these two books, we see judgment and grace coming together—judgment of our deeds and grace for those whose names are written in the book of life.

A great deal of angst arises among young people as a result of 20:14–15: 'Death and Hades were thrown into the lake of fire. This is the second death, the lake of fire; and anyone whose name was not found written in the book of life was thrown into the lake of fire.' When addressing the fears that young people have concerning this verse, we must remember the metaphorical nature of John's writing and contextualise it with the rest of scripture. In so doing, we are convinced that John is stressing the finality of judgment rather than its exact methodology. He is not portraying the reality of hell in 20:14 (note that Hades itself is thrown into the lake of fire, too). Instead, he is creating a parallel with what he will teach in the next chapter of Revelation. In chapter 21, he outlines a vision of fellowship in the city of God; in 20:14, he outlines a vision of fellowship that will be shared by lost human beings, the beast, the false prophet, the devil, Death and Hades. Again, we note that methodology is less important than implication. John intends to draw a distinction between the saved and the lost. As we disciple young people, we do not want them to react in fear to this verse. Rather, we want them to be inspired positively towards increased faith in a God who sits in glory on the throne of heaven. As a result, our young people will not run from the devil in fear. Instead, they will run towards God in joyful anticipation of salvation, which is the theme of our next chapter.

Some questions to consider

- How do your young people vocalise feelings of guilt and shame?
- Do your young people have a sense of judgment upon them? If so, what form does it take?
- In what ways can you creatively engage young people with the idea of final judgment without scaring them?
- If we recognise that Generation Y believers must not make peace with Babylon, how might you engage them creatively to consider their lifestyle choices and consumer choices? How can you unmask the powers of Babylon for your young people in a way that is meaningful for them?
- How might you engage Generation Y believers in the prophetic mission that lies before them?

Chapter 8

What is salvation?

Generation Y: the pursuit of happiness

Choice, in and of itself, is a core value for Generation Y. This is true, regardless of what the choice is and also regardless of the context in which the choice is to be made. For Generation Y, the value of 'choice' is at the root of happiness. The more choices young people have, the happier they believe themselves to be.

For many within Generation Y, therefore, the Christian understanding of salvation is countercultural and unacceptable because it appears to mark the end of choice. When we proclaim the gospel, young people are immediately disempowered by the idea that God has chosen them rather than that they have chosen God. As we disciple young people, we appear to be constantly closing down their opportunities to choose. We tell them that living the life of salvation is a lifestyle of obedience under the authority and power of God. That is often heard as the end of their ability to make choices, and so the gospel appears unattractive. To be effective in evangelising and discipling young people, we will need to help them discover the true meaning of 'choice'.

A central motif in Paul's letter to the Galatians is that, contrary to much understanding inherent within Generation Y, determinism and freedom are not polar opposites and, crucially, freedom and choice are not synonymous. What is required in the discipling of Generation Y believers is a reorientation of thought—an understanding that what is being pursued through their 'choices' is actually to be found only through our deterministic election by God to salvation. To put it more simply, what we all (Generation Y included) strive for through our choices is happiness, but the choices we make in life can lead only to impermanent happiness. Only God's choice for us can lead to ultimate happiness, which is salvation.

This understanding is theologically located in our understanding of what it means to be made in the *imago Dei*, the image of God. We are made in the *imago Dei* so that we can enjoy a life in relationship with him. In his book *On the Holy Spirit*, the 17th-century theologian John Owen wrote, 'Adam's soul was made meet and able to live to God, as his sovereign lord, chiefest good, and last end.' This was a notion based on Aristotelian teleology—the idea developed by Aristotle that the end (*telos*) to which we are all working is ultimate happiness. Everything we pursue as humans is geared towards the pursuit of ultimate happiness. This is not to suggest that every decision we make in life is filled with a profound realisation that ultimate happiness is what we seek! Instead, this pursuit is an often unspoken, and more often unrealised, driving force within us. As Aristotle wrote in his *Nicomachean Ethics*, 'We always choose [happiness] for its own sake and never for the sake of some other thing... nobody chooses happiness as a means of achieving... anything else whatsoever than just happiness... Happiness, then, is the end to which all our conscious acts are directed, is found to be final and self-sufficient.'

The prevailing spirit of Generation Y is that happiness is to be found through having the ability to choose, but the biblical witness is that human choice often leads to deep unhappiness and is therefore, in and of itself, not the pathway to true and lasting happiness. Instead, God's choosing of us—God's gracious gift of salvation—is the only means of finding such happiness. As Jesus said in John 10:10, 'I have come in order that you might have life— life in all its fullness' (GNB) For that reason, it is God's gracious gift of salvation that is the source of our true happiness.

We are to disciple Generation Y believers into the realisation that obedience to God does not mean the end of choice but that choices made within the strictures of a salvation lifestyle are the only means to attain what they truly seek—ultimate happiness. Too often, Christianity is perceived by the young to be a never-ending list of 'dos and don'ts', with the emphasis firmly on the 'don'ts', but we are not in a salvation relationship with God through our obedience to rules and regulations. We are in a salvation relationship because God has chosen us to live with him. To that end, the *imago Dei* within us is constructed such that we are able to make choices that draw us ever closer to God. So living out the life of holiness, the life of salvation, is a participation in who we are as created in the *imago Dei*. The life of salvation is therefore not the end of choice. It is the ultimate choice to be true to ourselves and to become the people we were destined to be. We were created in the *imago Dei*; we were destined for life in all its fullness. Salvation through holy choices is our beginning and our end. Convincing Generation Y believers of this most amazing truth will have a transformative impact on their ability to persevere with God as they seek to live out a countercultural approach to the notion of 'choice' among their peers.

It is not surprising that John has much to say about the idea of salvation in Revelation. His approach to this topic is particularly useful for our discipling efforts with Generation Y because he develops a dual understanding of salvation as a present experience and salvation as a future hope. These both accord with the needs of this current generation of young people. At the heart of this dual understanding is a single, gracious invitation that issues from the very throne of God.

God's plan for salvation

Three words in Revelation 4:1 record the whole intent of God: 'Come up here.' That is the invitation of the God of heaven to those of us on earth: we are to join him there. To that end, God initiated a plan of salvation for the whole of creation.

In John's vision, that plan is contained in a scroll, as he outlines in chapter 5. The scene opens in 5:1: 'And I saw in the right hand of him seated on the throne a scroll written within and on the back, having been sealed with seven seals.'* There are examples from the Old Testament of God giving prophetic writings on a scroll—for example, to Ezekiel and Daniel. The fact that the scroll in John's vision is sealed gives it an air of importance, as if it is a legal document. Here, in the right hand of God, is a legally binding account of the future destiny of his created order. The comprehensive nature of God's plan is confirmed by the fact that the scroll is written 'within and on the back'. Given the nature of the contents, it is not surprising that John exclaims in verse 3, 'No one was able in heaven or upon earth or under the earth to unroll the scroll or look into it.'* Since this is a legal document, the opening of the scroll indicates the enacting of what is written there. For that reason, no one can open it, because only God can put into effect the will of God. Accordingly, the divinity of Christ is affirmed in verse 5, in which one of the elders proclaims, 'The Lion from the tribe of Judah, the root of David, has won the victory so can unroll the scroll and its seven seals.'* This is a verse that brings deep encouragement. Through the victory of Christ, the plan of salvation for the world can be rolled out.

John's description of the Messiah in verse 6 details how the victory has been won. He writes, 'And I saw in the midst of the throne... a lamb standing as if it had been slain.'* These few words describe the most incredible theological truth. The Lamb is, of course, Jesus Christ the Messiah, who was slaughtered. We would expect an animal that had been slaughtered to be lying down, but this slaughtered lamb is standing. He has been resurrected. In one incredible sentence, we have the crucifixion and the resurrection portrayed before us as the slaughtered lamb standing. This is the foundation upon which God's plan for salvation is built. The crucified and resurrected Lamb of God has won the victory of life over death, and for that reason he stands in the midst of the throne in glory.

Elsewhere, John reminds us that this plan for salvation has been the foundation of God's relationship with humanity for all eternity. In Revelation 1:5–6, he writes, 'To the one who loves us and loosed us from our sins by his blood, and made us a kingdom, priests to his God and father, to him be glory and might for ever. Amen.'* We are reminded here of the exodus story in which the people of Israel were set free from the yoke of slavery under the Egyptians, as well as the Old Testament sacrifices that were fulfilled in the blood of Christ shed on the cross. As a result of that shed blood, we are priests—not like the Levite priestly order, which was reserved for just a few, but a new order of priesthood in which we can all share.

The response of heaven to this plan of salvation is recorded in Revelation 5:8: 'And when he took the scroll, the four living creatures and the twenty-four elders fell before the lamb each having a harp and golden bowls full of incense.'* The worship of God is the only possible response to the sacrificial death and resurrection of Jesus Christ, by which the plan of salvation is brought to reality. Encouraging participation in the worship of God must be at the very heart of our discipling activity with young people.

Salvation as a present experience

Having thought about the means of salvation, we now come to consider the issue of how we are to live out the life of salvation. It is clear from scripture that salvation is both a present experience and a future hope. Through John's metaphors of the 144,000 and the great multitude (Revelation 7 and 14), we encounter five ideas about what it means to live out our salvation in the everyday.

First, salvation is experienced when we submit our lives to God. Chapter 7 opens with four angels holding back the four winds of the

earth. In verse 3, another angel cries out, 'Do not harm the earth or
the sea or the trees until we have sealed the slaves of our God upon
their foreheads.'* By using the word *doulos* ('slave') rather than
diakonos ('servant'), John conveys the idea of utter devotion and
complete submission to God. Unlike a servant, the slave forgoes
all personal rights, ambition and even identity. The seal of salvation
is put on those who are utterly devoted to God, those who have
given their life over to him and find their true identity in him. This
is confirmed by the verb tense of 'until we have sealed', which, in
Greek, indicates an event that may or may not happen, depending
on the response of the individual. Whether or not a person is
sealed for salvation depends in part on how that person responds
to God. This is a stark reminder that, when we are discipling young
people, we must encourage them to be wholehearted in their walk
with God rather than complacent in their faith.

Second, salvation is experienced when we are rooted in Christ.
When the tribes of Israel are listed in 7:5–8, they begin with Judah.
This is the only time in the Bible when Judah heads up the list.
We know that Jesus descended from the tribe of Judah, so John is
making a theological point here about who is head of the Church.
The starting point of our salvation, metaphorically, is the man from
the tribe of Judah, and we must ensure that our young people have
him as the head of their spiritual ancestry.

Third, salvation is experienced when we do not engage in
idolatry. In the list of tribes, there is no mention of Dan. That tribe
has been replaced in verse 6 with Manasseh, which was actually
a sub-section of the tribe of Joseph. In Jewish theology, Dan
represents idolatry. In Numbers 2:25, we are told that Dan dwelt
in the north, and, just as blessings are supposed to come from the
east, so it was thought that spiritual darkness came from the north.
In addition, 1 Kings 12 tells how, when King Jeroboam tried to get
the people to worship his golden calves, the only ones persuaded
were the tribe of Dan. Young people in this generation are often
tempted into idolatry, often by putting possessions, ambitions or

even relationships before their faith in God. Effective discipling involves helping them to review their priorities in life, ensuring that God comes first.

Fourth, salvation is an experience offered by God to all. In Revelation 7:9, John says, 'I looked, and behold a great multitude, which no one was able to count, from every nation and tribe and people and language standing before the throne and before the lamb.'* This multitude is the fulfilment of God's promise to Abraham in Genesis 15:5: 'Look up at the heavens and count the stars—if indeed you can count them... So shall your offspring be' (NIV). In answer to the question of the multitude's identity in Revelation 7:13, the elder tells John, 'They are the ones who have come out of the great tribulation and washed their robes and made them white in the blood of the lamb' (v. 14*). According to the promises of God in 3:4 and 5:9, that means all of us who have persevered in the faith. The great multitude is therefore the universal Church, with every nation, tribe, people and language included. As we disciple young people, we must give them a sense of the scope of the mission field that lies before them.

Fifth, salvation is experienced when we are courageous in our witness to God. In 14:4, John gives a further description of the 144,000: 'These are the ones who have not defiled themselves with women, for they are virgins. These are the ones who follow the lamb wherever he goes. They have been redeemed from among people, first fruits to God and to the lamb, and in their mouths is found no lie, for they are unblemished.'* This is a complex metaphor that draws on three distinct Old Testament images. The image of ceremonial sexual purity comes from Deuteronomy, 1 Samuel and 2 Samuel, where men preparing to go to war in the name of God would abstain from sexual relations as a sign of their single-minded commitment to God's cause. Then there is the idea of first fruits: in Exodus 23:16, the first fruits of the harvest were dedicated to God, set apart for him as his rightful possession. The word 'unblemished' reminds us of the sacrificial lambs offered to God by the priests (for example,

Leviticus 23:12). When these three images are put together, John is painting a vivid picture of the need to be single-minded, set apart and sacrificial in our dedication to God's cause. We cannot effectively disciple young people if we portray Christianity as a Sunday hobby. It demands courage and perseverance to live out the life of salvation that God offers each one of us.

Salvation as a future hope

In 1 Corinthians 13:13, Paul confirmed faith, hope and love as the eternal values that remain. That being the case, it is crucial for us to give hope to the young people we disciple. Since hope is inextricably bound up with salvation, we must focus not only on the possibility that God can transform their present experience but also on the fact that eternal salvation is waiting for us as a future hope. This is not 'pie-in-the-sky-when-you-die' theology but a firm reality born out of the historical achievement of Jesus Christ, who died, was raised and ascended to heaven. In Revelation, John has much to say about salvation as a future hope. We can only explore a few central themes here.

First, we note that our eternal salvation is a gift from God. In his vision of heaven in 15:2, John states that the redeemed stand 'with harps of God in their hands'. We are pictured playing and singing a song of deliverance, but it is important to note that the means of playing has been given to us by God. It is not my harp or your harp. It is God's harp given to us. Therefore, we have not earned deliverance ourselves but have been given it as a gift. For that reason, we must disciple young people into an attitude of thanksgiving for the salvation that God gives to them. Out of that thankful disposition arise true worship and a life of commitment as they await their future salvation.

Second, we note that our eternal salvation marks the end of all dualistic tensions. We have seen previously that many of the psychological and emotional difficulties faced by young people are a result of the tension of identity formation: they are citizens of heaven but also citizens on earth. Dualisms are at the heart of so much angst for teenagers: they are too young to be treated like adults but too old to behave like children, too young to make lifestyle choices but too old to drift along in a state of irresponsibility, too immature to handle deep relationships but too old to be naïve in friendship formations, and so on. If dualism disappeared, teenage angst would be eradicated.

The good news of eternal salvation is that it is a non-dualistic experience. In 21:1–3, John says:

And I saw a new heaven and a new earth. For the first heaven and the first earth has departed and the sea is no more. And I saw the holy city, the new Jerusalem, coming down out of heaven from God, prepared as a bride made beautiful for her husband. And I heard a loud voice from the throne saying, 'Behold, the dwelling of God is with humanity, and he shall dwell with them, and they shall be his people, and God himself shall be with them.' *

This is not to suggest that the old heaven and the old earth are completely eradicated, any more than the old covenant was eradicated when Jesus declared the wine to represent 'the new covenant in my blood' (Luke 22:20). Similarly, our flesh does not cease to exist in the light of Paul's teaching in 2 Corinthians 5:17 that 'if anyone is in Christ, they are a new creation; the old has gone, behold the new has come'.* Rather, in all these examples there is continuity between the old and the new, a complete renewal of the old rather than a replacement of it. The old and the new now exist as one; there is no longer any old and there is no longer any new. The dualism between old and new has collapsed and all has become one.

This happens in salvation for one specific reason. It is a central feature of our fallen world that we view everything through dualisms—up/down, in/out, good/bad, backwards/forwards, him/

her, black/white and so on—but dualisms only exist because they put ego at the centre. The ceiling is only 'up' in relation to me; the floor is only 'down' in relation to me; the trees are only 'outside' in relation to where I stand, and so on. Dualism exists only when the ego is central, and the ego is central only as a result of our fallen state of being. When our ego is displaced, all dualisms disappear. So when John describes the new reality in Revelation 21, all dualisms have vanished because God, not our ego, is at the centre. For that reason, John is able to declare that 'the sea is no more'. Earlier, we thought about the sea as a metaphor for chaos. Where there are no dualisms, where ego is not the central focus, there is no more chaos and confusion. Now that is something for young people to anticipate eagerly! Crucially, in 21:3, there is no longer any separation between God and humanity: heaven and earth become truly intertwined. The ultimate dualism—the separation between God and humanity—has been collapsed, which is the very definition of salvation.

Third, as dualisms collapse, all negativity is eradicated. In 21:4, John says, 'He shall wipe every individual tear out of their eyes, and death shall be no more, or sorrow, or crying in grief or pain.'* This is such a beautiful verse to meditate upon with young people. The image of God lovingly removing every tear from our eyes can almost be seen as an evocative suggestion of the tear ducts being removed. Such is the eradication of negativity that we will have no cause to cry or feel sorrow.

Fourth, as negativity is eradicated, so eternal salvation marks the dissipation of the power of sin. For those who experience salvation, there is a metaphorical return to Eden before the fall. In 22:1–2, John writes:

And he showed me the river of the water of life, bright as crystal, flowing out of the throne of God and of the lamb. In the middle of the street and on both sides of the river, is a tree of life with twelve fruits, yielding its fruit each month, and the fruit of the tree is for the healing of the nations.

113

This draws our minds back to Genesis 2:9–10, where we read, 'In the middle of the Garden [of Eden] were the tree of life and the tree of the knowledge of good and evil. A river watering the Garden flowed from Eden.'* At the end, as at the beginning, a tree of life settles peaceably on the banks of a flowing river. But there is also a reference to Ezekiel 47, in which the prophet's vision of a restored temple is outlined:

Fruit trees of all kinds will grow on both banks of the river. Their leaves will not wither, nor will their fruit fail. Every month they will bear, because the water from the sanctuary flows to them. Their fruit will serve for food and their leaves for healing. (v. 12, NIV)

Fifth, eternal salvation is the promise of intimacy with God. In Revelation 22:4, John says, 'They will see his face, and his name will be upon their foreheads' (NIV). The idea of seeing God's face is perhaps the most intimate expression of relationship that scripture affords to us. In Exodus 33:20 and 23, God told Moses, 'You cannot see my face, for no one may see me and live… You will see my back; but my face must not be seen' (NIV). Even Moses, then, was denied the right to see the face of God, but here in the new Jerusalem the experience of salvation is hallmarked by a face-to-face relationship, suggesting that we shall know the character of God in fullness. Furthermore, the idea of God's name being on our foreheads suggests that the worship and service of God will be our every thought and will consume us in its glory. In Exodus 28:36–38, we are told that the high priest made a plate of pure gold and wrote on it 'Holy to the Lord' before placing it on his forehead. In the new Jerusalem, each one of us will engage in priestly worship in the service of God.

If Generation Y is marked out by its pursuit of happiness, then the prospect of eternal salvation is the greatest gift we can offer young people as we seek to disciple them in the faith. As they hold in mind the future glory that awaits them, so their present experience will be transformed and they will mature in faith and in the likeness of the glory of Christ. That is surely what we long to see among the young people we serve.

Some questions to consider

- In a postmodern world, how can we creatively engage young people with the idea that there has been a plan for salvation from all eternity?
- How do the young people you work with understand their place within the plan and purposes of God? What do they need to hear from you in this regard?
- What would it look like for your young people truly to submit their lives to the service of God? What impact would it have on your local church and local community?
- How might you encourage young people to develop spiritual disciplines so that they become more deeply rooted in Christ?
- What idolatries are prevalent among your young people? How might you creatively challenge them and replace them with a vision of God?
- What concepts do your young people hold concerning an eternity with God? What images can you creatively use that might deepen their faith and hope for the future?
- What dualisms cause emotional and psychological difficulties for the young people you work with? How might you help them overcome the tensions they create?

Chapter 9

How important are worship and prayer?

Generation Y: a people of praise

Leading young people into a life of worship must be the very heart of our desire when it comes to discipling Generation Y. The life of worship is our ultimate destiny as human beings. We were created for the sole purpose of spending time in God's presence and glorifying his name. It is significant that, in the Genesis creation story, human beings were created on the sixth day immediately prior to the seventh day, which is the sabbath. The sabbath day is the only one of the seven that never ends: there is no declaration, 'Evening passed and morning came—that was the seventh day.' This seventh day, on which God rests in the company of humanity, is ever open and never ending. We are still living in the seventh day, and its purpose is that we can eternally rest with God in a relationship of mutual love and our adoration of him.

Engaging young people in the worship life of the church is always difficult. However, there are particular difficulties for those who are nurturing and discipling Generation Y believers. This is the age of the celebrity, the age of mass entertainment. It is very difficult to avoid the temptation of creating worship experiences that are little more than entertainment extravaganzas. Too often, the medium swamps the message. While this may make for positive numerical growth, it will do little for spiritual depth. The temptation to turn worship into entertainment is further fuelled by the fact that Generation Y believers often treat worship as a consumer choice. More often than not, young people will attend a church where they find their needs met through the worship; receiving individual fulfilment is deemed to be more important than exercising gifts for the sake of others. This is not to be despised, of course. All young people, of whatever generation, have always pursued happiness, drawn to the place and community that most clearly offers it to them.

The challenge that lies before those of us who are discipling young people in this generation, then, is to help them recognise worship as the pursuit of authenticity, not personal contentment. The two are not necessarily the same. Since the sabbath experience of living in relationship with God is what we were created for, we discover who we truly are as we worship. For that reason, worship can be a painful encounter just as much as a time of joy. The psalmists knew this, so it is important for us to introduce young people to the Psalms as a coherent and holistic resource for worship and personal devotion.

The worship of the Father, in the power of the Holy Spirit, for what he has done for us through the atoning death of the Son, is a constant motif throughout the New Testament. However, John's Revelation does give a unique perspective on worship—namely the cosmic nature of the act. In Revelation, we are confronted by the spectacle of the whole of creation, throughout all time and space, caught up together in the worship of the Creator God. Revelation is infused with images that portray the sheer size and intensity of worship to a degree not mirrored anywhere else in scripture. Furthermore, Revelation leads us into a deeper understanding of why we worship the Father, as well as the importance and responsibility of engaging in prayer. These are crucial themes to explore with young people, particularly those who may feel disillusioned or despondent about local experiences of worship in small or declining churches. It is a real gift to introduce them to the reality of worship that both incorporates and transcends their personal experience, contained within the four walls of their current setting. Generation Y long to be part of something bigger. By discipling them into the reality of worship as perceived by John, we can help them to achieve that longing.

The song of salvation

In Revelation 5:9, John describes in his vision the heavenly worship of God and introduces it with an interesting phrase: 'And they sang a new song' (NIV). This is a phrase used in the Psalms that always relates to celebrating the mercy of God and his deliverance from distress and suffering. For example, Psalm 40:1–3 says, 'I waited patiently for the Lord; he turned to me and heard my cry. He lifted me out of the slimy pit, out of the mud and mire; he set my feet on a rock and gave me a firm place to stand. He put a new song in my mouth, a hymn of praise to our God' (NIV). Again, Psalm 98:1 says, 'Sing to the Lord a new song, for he has done marvellous things; his right hand and his holy arm have worked salvation for him' (NIV). Therefore, the worship of God is primarily a response to the mercy and compassion of God, experienced through his acts of salvation.

This is most clearly evidenced in Revelation 19. In verse 1, God is praised because of the nature of his judgments: 'Hallelujah! Salvation and glory and power belong to our God, for true and just are his judgments' (NIV). As we noted in an earlier chapter, it is through God's judgment that salvation comes to the world. This is a constant theme throughout Revelation. The redeemed host beside the sea of glass in 15:3 sing, 'Just and true are your ways' (NIV), while the martyrs beneath the altar in 16:7 proclaim, 'True and just are your judgments' (NIV). There is nothing capricious about God's judgment. It is just and it is true because it is a response to the two sins of corrupting the earth and martyring God's servants. For this reason, God is worthy of our worship and praise.

The praise continues but, in 19:3, the focus shifts a little: 'Hallelujah; her smoke rises for ever and ever.' Here, the cry of 'Hallelujah!' indicates that the destruction of civilisation opposed to God, symbolised by the smoke rising, goes on for ever and ever. By this is announced the new world order. The old has gone and the new is coming. As we disciple young people into a deeper understanding of worship, we must help them to locate their praise within this moment of cosmic transition. Essentially, our worship looks forward to the time when God's glory will be fully revealed. There is a sense in which our worship now is a prophetic act, announcing that which is to come. It is for this reason that the Eucharist is at the very heart of Christian worship. Through that commemoration meal, time is contracted into a single moment as we proclaim together, 'Christ has died, Christ is risen, Christ will come again.'

Ultimately, however, our worship is a proclamation of the sovereignty and authority of the God who saves. As such, there is a missionary intent as well as a devotional intent that young people must grasp with regard to worship. In Revelation 19:6, the shout of praise goes forth: 'Hallelujah! For our Lord God Almighty reigns' (NIV). God has judged, the old has gone, the new is coming and, as a result, the Lord God has entered into his reign. That is the great proclamation of the Church, not just in the future but in the here and now, too. That is the gospel, the good news that our young people are called to proclaim. As Jesus said in Mark 1:15, 'The kingdom of God has come near.'

The missiological intent of worship is strengthened in Revelation 19:7 with an imperative that encourages us all to recognise the glory of God: 'Let us rejoice and exult and give him the glory.' The reason for giving him the glory is that he has brought us salvation. This is clear from the very nuanced comment in verse 7 that 'the marriage of the lamb has come and his wife has made herself ready'. It is a crucial nuance that John does not use the word for 'bride', which is *numphein*. Instead, he uses the word for 'wife', which is *gune*. In 21:2, John refers to the people of God as a bride, but here in 19:7 the vision is of 'the other side' of the final judgment. Before the final judgment, we are the bride of Christ being prepared for an eternity with him, but after the final judgment, we will be the wife of Christ, married to him and enjoying the closest possible union. This beautiful metaphor of salvation underpins the worship of God's people and must act as a motivation for mission during the current age. As we are reminded in 19:9, 'Blessed are those who are invited to the marriage banquet of the lamb.'* This is the mission imperative: we are not worthy of an eternity with God. We are there by invitation only. It is part of our worship to proclaim the invitation of God to others, and we must encourage our young people to participate in this mission activity.

Salvation is not merely an individualistic experience, of course. Through the cross of Christ, the whole of creation is redeemed. That being the case, we are reminded in 5:13 that the entire created order participates in worship, in the song of salvation. The fact that the glory of God is revealed through the redemption of creation is most clearly demonstrated in the song of praise recorded in 4:11: 'You are worthy, our Lord and God, to receive the glory and the honour and the power, for you created all things and through your will they were created and have their being.'* The verb 'to receive' here, *labein*, is in a tense that indicates a single action complete within itself. We are tempted to read this verse as meaning that God receives, continuously, glory and honour and power through our worship, but that is an erroneous reading. Instead, it is saying that there will be a single act through which he will receive glory and honour and power. Given the rest of the verse, that single act has something to do with creation. What is being hinted at here is that one day, when Christ returns, the whole of creation will be restored and renewed and, in that act of restoration and renewal, the name of God will be glorified.

As we disciple young people into a life of worship, we must help them to develop this cosmic perspective. They do not worship solely because they are saved. They worship in the company of the angels and archangels and all the company of heaven, for ever praising him and singing, 'Holy, holy, holy'. They worship him in the knowledge that all creation will one day be restored and the glory and power of God will be visible for all to see. This is a vision of worship beyond all comprehension! If, through our discipling endeavours, we can encourage our young people to gain even a glimpse of this eternal act of worship, we will go some way towards facilitating an incredible transformation that will have an extraordinary impact in their lives. This is why we must dissuade young people from being consumers of worship. Worship cannot be assessed by its 'entertainment value'. Instead, we must instil in them a theological understanding of what is happening in and through worship, and Revelation can help us to do that.

Purity in worship

Our God is holy, pure and jealous. It is his right to demand purity of worship from us. This is a difficult notion for Generation Y believers, who often judge worship by its entertainment value or creativity. Often, creativity is mistaken for purity. While it is important to have worship that engages young people, this must never become the measure of its appropriateness. Purity in worship is a priority that far exceeds creative engagement. The demand of God in this regard is made very clear in Revelation.

In the letter to the church at Thyatira, we read, 'But I have this against you, that you tolerate the woman Jezebel, who calls herself a prophetess and teaches and deceives my slaves, leading them into sexual immorality and the eating of food sacrificed to idols' (2:20*). There is an element of metaphor here, calling to mind the story in 2 Kings 9 where Jezebel was accused of sexual immorality and sorcery. She met a very nasty end: having been thrown out of a window, her corpse was eaten by dogs, leaving only the skull, hands and feet on the street. Jezebel is being used as a metaphor for those who are leading the Thyatirans astray into impure worship.

The word used here for 'sexual immorality' is *porneia*. Scripture is very clear about what makes a particular sexual act unlawful. It is an act that contravenes the teachings of the Torah, the first five books of the Old Testament. In the Torah, only two sexual acts are condemned—commercial sex and what we call cultic sex, which is the use of prostitutes in religious acts of worship. That being the case, what Jesus is condemning here are practices in worship that are abhorrent to God. This is not a critique of sexual ethics; it is a critique of false worship—practices in worship that go against what is right for our God. If we do not worship in purity, we are being unfaithful to God. We are reminded of the story of Hosea in the Old Testament, who was commanded to act out the unfaithfulness of the people of Israel to God by marrying Gomer. God will not tolerate impurity in worship: 'Behold, I am throwing her on to a bed and those who commit adultery with her into great suffering if they do not repent of their deeds. And her children I will kill to death' (2:22–23*). There is such finality about the phrase 'killed to death'. God finds impure worship abhorrent and is fiercely angry about it.

However, a wonderful promise is given in 2:26, 28 to those who do not indulge in impure worship: 'I will give to [them] authority over the nations… and I will give to [them] the morning star.'* In these two metaphors, we are offered a share in the authority of God. Just as the prophecy of Psalm 2 was fulfilled when the Father gave authority over the nations to the Son, so we who remain pure in worship shall share that gift. The same promise is made with reference to the morning star, which, in Greek mythology, is Venus. In Babylonian mythology, Venus represents sovereignty. In Roman mythology, Venus represents sovereignty and victory, which is the reason why so many Roman generals built temples to Venus after they had won their battles. God abhors impure worship and is angry with those who lead Christians astray. He will come in judgment on such people, but to those who resist and persevere, he will give authority to rule.

This passage challenges us to think afresh about how we disciple young people into purity of worship. We do not use temple prostitutes and we do not eat food sacrificed to idols but we must always be sure that our worship is pleasing to God. In Exodus 20:5, we are reminded, 'I the Lord your God am a jealous God.' He will tolerate no rivals and he wants to be worshipped in purity, love and truth. We must be constantly examining our worship to make sure that it is a worthy offering to our holy and sovereign God. We must constantly search our hearts and minds to make sure that our attitude towards worship is pleasing to him. Too often, our complacency in worship sets a bad example to those we are seeking to disciple. Revelation 2 serves as a reminder that we must take our worship of God very seriously, both for our own sakes and for the young people we are discipling.

The power of prayer

Mentoring young people into a life of prayer is absolutely at the heart of our discipling endeavours. There is much that can be said about this, but we are limited in this book to what we can learn from Revelation about the power of prayer. Given this boundary, there are two particular points upon which we can reflect.

First, we must convince our young people that their prayers are very precious to God. In Revelation 8:3, we are told, 'Another angel came and took his place upon the altar having a golden censer, and much incense was given to him, in order that he may add to the prayers of all the saints on the golden altar before the throne.'* The fact that the angel 'took his place' indicates that there was something preordained about this action; it was designed to be that way. In contrast to 5:8, where the incense *is* the prayers of the saints, here the incense is offered *with* the prayers of the saints. It is a subtle difference but the message of 8:3 is that the prayers of humans are offered to God with the incense of angels. That being the case, we are reminded of just how valuable our prayers are. They come before God with 'much incense' and are laid on a golden altar, a symbol of great worth. That is very encouraging for the young people we are discipling. They may feel that their prayers sometimes make little difference. Perhaps they are too embarrassed to waste God's time with seemingly petty requests, but it is a great encouragement that, every time they pray, an angel carries that prayer to the throne of God, incense is wafted in heaven, and the prayer is left before the throne on a golden altar. If this image does not transform the way they view their prayers, nothing will!

Second, we must help our young people to gain a sense of responsibility concerning their prayers. This is not necessarily a comfortable truth, but we have a duty to teach it all the same. In 8:5, we read, 'The angel took the censer and filled it up with the fire of the altar and threw it on to the earth, and there was thunder and loud noises and lightning and an earthquake.'* What we have here is the beginnings of the pouring out of the judgments of God—in response to the prayers of the saints. This is a complex reality for us to comprehend but the truth is that God brings his judgments to the earth as a response to our prayers. In 6:10, the saints under the altar cried out, 'Sovereign Lord, holy and true, how long will it be before you judge and avenge our blood on the inhabitants of the earth?' These were the prayers of the martyrs, asking God to do what was right and justify his sovereignty in the light of unrighteousness on earth.

Perhaps we can summarise that prayer in three words: 'Your kingdom come.' That is what we pray regularly, if not daily, in the Lord's Prayer. It is a phrase that rolls off our lips very easily. It becomes a habit for us; we give little thought to what we are saying, but it is the most powerful prayer-phrase in the world. When we pray, 'Your kingdom come', we are asking God to bring judgment on ungodliness in the world, to cleanse the cosmos from all that is antichrist and to bring his reign to absolute completion. We need to take responsibility for the fact that, when we pray 'Your kingdom come', we are actually praying for the intensification and final completion of every spiritual battle in the cosmos. These are not trite words. We need to take responsibility for what we pray and encourage our young people to do the same. When we say, 'Your kingdom come', that prayer is carried up to heaven and, with the incense of the angels, laid on a golden altar before the throne of God. If we do not want God to act on it, we should not pray it. We must realise that God's acting on it will inevitably mean the bringing of judgment as well as salvation.

Worship in spirit and in truth

Worship is not a consumer choice or an entertainment event. Worship is nothing less than the fulfilment of our destiny as human beings. While it is always right to create opportunities for worship that are culturally useful, it is a mistake to create opportunities for worship that are only culturally relevant. The worship of the Father, in the power of the Spirit, for his act of salvation through the Son, is something that both incorporates and transcends culture. Focusing too much on the incorporated culture may lead to a diminishing of the transcendent experience.

Generation Y has enough opportunities to enjoy entertainment. Young people do not need the church to entertain them. The role of those who are discipling young people today must always be to guide them in ways that dissolve their culture into the transcendent realm, which is the coming together of the whole created order in the worship of God. This is a hugely important activity, which must go beyond entertainment value. In this act, young people explore God and, in so doing, find themselves. They learn to look beyond themselves and recognise, perhaps for the first time, their innate connectedness with the created order through time and space. They recognise the part they must play in the unfolding drama and story that is God's future. If we can disciple young people into this depth of self-awareness and awareness of the Other, then we will have truly fulfilled our ministry to them.

Some questions to consider

- If you had to choose three words to describe worship in your local church, what would they be?
- How do your young people view worship in the local church?
- How might you creatively engage young people with the truth that, when they worship, they are part of a cosmic movement of praise?
- In the light of what you have read, how might you teach young people what it means to participate in the Eucharist as part of their worship?
- To what extent is the worship in your local church a missional act as well as an act of proclamation? What might be done to strengthen this aspect of worship?
- What does purity of worship look like in your context? How might you encourage your young people to take purity in worship more seriously?
- How can you help to develop the spiritual discipline of prayer in the lives of the young people you work with?
- How much of an emphasis is there on prayer in your own life? How might you strengthen it?

Chapter 10

How do I live as a disciple of Jesus?

Generation Y: the challenge to commit

We often hear Baby Boomers complain, 'Young people today have no commitment.' That is a false critique. Young people today are often very committed indeed. However, commitment among Generation Y looks very different from commitment among Baby Boomers, Generation X and, particularly, the Silent Generation. For the Baby Boomers and the Silent Generation in particular, commitment meant signing up for something and sticking at it through thick and thin. Employment mobility was not an issue for these generations: a job was for life. Divorce rates were much lower for these generations: a marriage was for life. But commitment does not look like this for Generation Y.

Generation Y commitment has less to do with longevity and more to do with depth. A young person may not hold down a job for very long but, as long as they are in that employment, they are likely to give it their all. The same is true of relationships. Generation Y relationships tend to be hallmarked by absolute loyalty. That is why the breakdown of a friendship can be so devastating for young people today. Friendship groups will be deeply affected by the disloyalty of one member against another. Disloyalty will not be tolerated and a young person may become socially isolated through an act of betrayal, however innocuous it may have seemed to the offender. It may be redeemable within the context of an ordinary friendship group, but the consequences of disloyalty for a gang member and their family can be tragic.

Generally speaking, we observe that Generation Y exhibits an optimism mirroring that of the Baby Boomers. Many young people are looking for a cause to commit to but do not trust the machinery of society, whether political or religious. As we seek to disciple Generation Y, we can be encouraged that a desire to commit is part of its DNA. From a faith perspective, once a young person commits to Christ, we can be fairly sure that, with appropriate nurturing, the commitment will be long lasting, but the challenge that faces us is simply this: Generation Y will only commit to something that is worth committing to. If young people cannot see the benefits, they will not make the commitment.

Commitment is part of identity formation. Young people learn who they are by what they commit to. For that reason, commitment to church is likely to be one of a number of options being explored at any given time. Those of us who are nurturing young people in faith find that we are competing for their interest and time against a range of other possible activities. It is an unspoken fear within Generation Y that firm commitment to one activity will provide a depth of identity-definition that is too restrictive. Why be defined as a Christian when there are so many other exciting possibilities to explore?

It is, then, both the greatest challenge and the greatest act of liberation to disciple young people so that they form their identity in Christ. The truth of the gospel is that we discover who we truly are—we discover our destiny—only when we are in the presence of Christ. That was the experience of John on Patmos. When confronted by his vision of Christ, he was completely overawed: 'When I saw him, I fell at his feet as though dead' (1:17), and there are similar responses recorded elsewhere in scripture (see, for example, Joshua 5:14; Daniel 10:7–9; Ezekiel 1:28). However, God does not want us to be paralysed by fear when we encounter him. Jesus' response to John in Revelation 1:17 was beautiful: 'And he placed his hand on me, saying, "Do not fear."'* A reassuring touch from God was required because he had a ministry for John to fulfil.

In similar fashion, God has a ministry for each of the young people we are discipling. Ultimately, our mentoring efforts are all about preparing young people to make a firm commitment to Jesus and fulfil their destiny in him. It is a really tough task because our young people are fighting against such self-definition. However, once they see how attractive a destiny in Christ can be, they are likely to want to 'go deep' with him. Then, if we portray Christianity as only one lifestyle option among many, they will become disillusioned and walk away, but if we portray discipleship as a radical lifestyle that requires real courage and depth, we can be sure that their commitment will stand. Discipling Generation Y demands that we walk closely alongside young people as they explore depth of commitment to Christ and what it will entail. Revelation provides us with five key principles that will underpin longevity of commitment and constancy in ministry in young people as they find their way with God.

Young disciples must learn to pace themselves

The passion of youth is powerful. Young disciples want to change the world, which is laudable, but they want to change the world today. It is hard to persuade them that they may need to wait until next week! As a result, we often see the flame of youthful discipleship burn out before it has had a chance to shine brightly in the world. As we disciple young people, we must persuade them to pace themselves. The Christian faith is a marathon, not a sprint.

The church in Ephesus was renowned for its energetic passion. In Revelation 2:2, Jesus commends them by saying, 'I know your deeds, your toil and your perseverance.'* The word used here for toil, *kopos*, indicates practical labour and hectic activity. The

Ephesians worked hard for God but they were so intent on pursuing orthodox faith and practice that they had pushed themselves to the point of exhaustion. However, Jesus was not entirely happy with the Ephesian church: 'But I have against you that you have forsaken your first love' (v. 4*). The sad truth is that the Ephesians were so busy doing Christian things that they had neglected love for Christ, love for each other and love for the world.

This provides us with a deep moment of self-reflection as we consider how we model Christian discipleship to those whom we are nurturing in the faith. The forsaking of our first love creeps up on us over a period of time. We may be so busy at church, preparing so many sermons, going to so many prayer meetings, involving ourselves in so many youth groups and worship events and being on so many committees that we think we are doing it all out of love and commitment. Actually, though, over a period of time, the love has decreased and the activity has increased. If we get off the merry-go-round for just a moment, we see that love has very little to do with our motivation and that we are just caught up in a round of busyness. That's not where we started. Each one of us began out of a desire to love and to serve, but over time the motivation changed so imperceptibly that we cannot even pinpoint when it began to happen.

This is not the life to which Jesus has called us, and he gives us the option to right this wrong in our lives: 'Remember, therefore, from where you have fallen, and think differently, and do your first works' (2:5*). Of course, it would have been easy for the Ephesians to read this and then undertake a new type of activity. We are so geared up to activity that it is hard for us to think any differently, but the question is not 'What does God want me to *do* for him?' The question is 'What does God want me to *be* for him?' We must be sure to model that attitude to young people while also ensuring that they do not burn out through too much activity, too soon into their walk with Christ.

Young disciples must take responsibility for one another

To the church in Pergamum, Jesus said, 'I know where you live—where Satan has his throne' (Revelation 2:13, NIV). This is a deeply penetrating comment because the word used for 'you live', *katoikeis*, is in a verb tense that suggests that the Christians were settled down and quite happy to go about their everyday business in the place where Satan lived. Jesus wanted to stress their passivity in the face of all that was wrong where they lived and worshipped. It is certainly the case that Pergamum, with its many pagan temples, was a place of idolatry, and some of the Christians had stood against it. Antipas, named in verse 13 as a martyr for Christ, may have been a specific individual but, as the name in Greek means 'against all', it could be a metaphor for a group of courageous believers.

The critique of Jesus against the Christians in Pergamum comes in 2:14: 'You have some there who hold to the teaching of Balaam.' Jesus was saying that faithful Christians were living side by side with others who were professing the Christian faith while following false teaching. It seems that the faithful were quite happy to allow this situation to continue. There was, within the church at Pergamum, a level of liberalism that Jesus found deeply offensive. Christians were allowed to behave in such a way as to be a stumbling block to others without ever being challenged.

In essence, the Christians at Pergamum were not taking responsibility for one another. They had forgotten that faith is a community event rather than the decision of each individual. Their attitude was one of 'live and let live'. Since Generation Y is growing up in such an individualised society, it is intensely countercultural for us to stress the community aspect of the Christian faith. However, it is crucial that peer mentoring becomes part and parcel of the discipleship programme and lifestyle. As young people learn to hold one another to account in the faith, and learn to do so without judgment, so they will also develop the ability to reflect on their own walk with God. I mentioned above that loyalty and commitment to one another is in the DNA of Generation Y, but that characteristic co-exists alongside a deep sense of individualism. Those of us who are Baby Boomers or Generation X may find this paradox difficult to reconcile, but that is not the case with Generation Y. Those of us who are seeking to disciple young people today must not try to resolve the paradox of community versus individualism. It does not need to be resolved. Our task is merely to help young people prioritise the community over and above the individual. By so doing, we will not only help individual young people to go deep in faith; we will also help to create communities of faith that are attractive to other young people. They will see the level of commitment and loyalty of one person to another and will want to be a part of it. They may well seek to 'belong' before they 'believe', but that is a perfectly acceptable strategy for mission in the 21st century because it speaks deeply into the value base of Generation Y.

Young disciples must learn to be here now

Generation Y believers are awash with opportunities for memorable Christian worship experiences. Young Christians are spoilt for choice when it comes to mass gatherings, teaching events, retreats, charismatic 'happenings' and weekend conferences. Many Christian leaders are eager for their young people to participate in such opportunities, knowing that they will receive an injection of spiritual experience that is just not possible in their local church, and of course there are real benefits to such participation. The negative side, however, is that the young Christian may not learn how to find God in the everyday and will hark back to the spiritual high as the moment of deepest encounter with God. They will rely on the memory to sustain them in faith until the calendar rolls around and they can attend again in order to be recharged. This is no way to go deep with God.

The city of Sardis had an illustrious history. Constructed in the Hermus Valley on the side of a mountain, it seemed impregnable to attack. After an earthquake in AD17, it was soon rebuilt. Its reputation had been built on its quality carpet-making, and citizens were able to pan for gold in the Pactolus stream that flowed through its streets. Sardis stood rich, proud and self-sufficient, but this sense of pride was actually a grand exercise in self-deception. The reality was that Sardis was a city in decline. It lived on its past glories rather than focusing on the true situation in which it found itself.

Jesus' critique of the church in Sardis, recorded in Revelation 3:1–2, would have cut them to the quick: 'I know your works, that you have a reputation of being alive, but you are dead. Wake up.'* Like the city in which it dwelt, the church was reliant on past glories rather than relying on the Holy Spirit in the present day. It appeared to be a bustling church, much like Ephesus, but the power was gone. In the same way that a car that has run out of petrol can still move forward when it is on a slope but will eventually come to a standstill when the energy has dissipated, so the church was running on empty and moving towards a complete standstill. Jesus' critique was that it had become a shrine to the good old days and the Christians were living in memory lane.

We want young people to experience the 'spiritual high' that mass youth events can provide, but we do not want them to rely on such events as the energy for their discipleship. As we seek to mentor young people, our task is to help them find God in the here and now, not just in the memory of the last conference they attended. This is difficult to achieve if we think that our programme of discipleship must compete in terms of entertainment value, but it does not. Remember that Generation Y wants to 'go deep', and that can be achieved only by finding God in the mundane elements of everyday living. By all means, encourage your young people to experience being part of something bigger at Christian festivals, but do not encourage them to replace the real work of daily Christian discipleship with these occasions. Young Christians must learn how to 'be here now' with God.

Young disciples must stay passionate for God

Being a Christian is not just a Sunday hobby. If we have learnt one thing from our study of Revelation, it is that Jesus wants absolute commitment and wholehearted discipleship from those who confess his name. We cannot play at being a Christian. We have already commented on how Generation Y knows what it is to express commitment, particularly in relationships. At the heart of the discipling process must be an endeavour to help young people stay passionate about God. Once the passion fades, the life of discipleship is in tatters.

In 3:15–16, Jesus issues the church in Laodicea with a stinging rebuke: 'I know your deeds, that you are neither cold nor boiling hot. I wish you were either cold or boiling hot. Since you are lukewarm and neither boiling hot nor cold, I am about to vomit you out of my mouth.'* The Laodiceans would have immediately understood the metaphor. The waters in the springs of Colosse, where their sister church was, ran pure and icy cold. The waters in the rivers and springs of the Hierapolis, geographically nearby, ran boiling hot, like geysers. But the rivers and springs from Laodicea, Asopus and Caprus, were lukewarm and tepid, full of limescale. What a terrible comparison to draw with their faith! The cold waters of Colosse brought refreshment, but the Laodicean church couldn't provide that. The hot waters of the Hierapolis brought healing, but the Laodicean church couldn't provide that either. They were lukewarm and full of spiritual limescale, clogging up the pipes of spirituality. This was a damning judgment from God. It is hard for us to hear that lukewarm Christians make Jesus sick to his stomach. It is hard to know what to do with such intensity of emotion, but we cannot rationalise this saying of Christ away or soften the blow. Jesus says what he means and he means what he says.

We may be discipling young people who respond with anxiety to this verse, but in his compassion Jesus offers a way forward to all who want to repent of their lukewarm approach to discipleship and rekindle their original passion. The gracious offer of Christ is in 3:20: 'Behold, I stand at the door and knock; if anyone hears my voice and opens the door, I will come in to them and will eat a meal with them and they with me.'* We must remember that this verse has nothing to do with an evangelistic call to faith: it is written to lukewarm Christians who need to rediscover their passion for God. The language Jesus uses reminds us of the last supper, the moment when Jesus shared a meal with those for whom he was about to die. We might, therefore, want to encourage our young people to share in the Eucharist regularly, so that they can re-enact their response to this call and reopen the door of their lives to Jesus. But this verse looks forward as well as backward. It also gives us hope for the supper that is to come: 'And I confer on you, just as my father conferred on me, a kingdom, so that you may eat and drink at my table in my kingdom' (Luke 22:29–30).

If you are ministering to a young person who feels anxious about lukewarm discipleship, this passage offers real hope. It is never too late to repent of complacency. Christ stands at the door and knocks. Once that door is reopened, the feasting can begin again.

Young disciples must be committed to mission

The thought of sharing the faith with peers and family, and even strangers, can be a frightening thought for young people. In an increasingly sceptical and secularised age, those involved in mission activity experience resistance. We are asking a lot from those we are mentoring when we ask them to engage in mission.

It is of real comfort, then, that Jesus had a message for the church in Philadelphia that was so weak and so vulnerable. For this fragile congregation, there was no angry word of critique, only a message of encouragement from their Saviour. It is interesting that Jesus encourages his weakest church to engage in the task of evangelism. We might have expected him to encourage Ephesus or Sardis towards this task—after all, they were numerically strong and of great reputation—but Jesus bypasses the strongest and entrusts the gospel message to the weakest. That, of course, encapsulates the values of the kingdom, in which the first are last and the last first, in which the weak are made strong.

In Revelation 3:8, Jesus states, 'I have given before you an open door, which no one is able to close.'* The idea of a door being open or shut is a common one in the scriptures and it always relates to mission opportunities. In Acts 14:27, when Paul and Barnabas are in Antioch, we read, 'They gathered the church together and reported all that God had done through them and how he had opened the door of faith to the Gentiles' (NIV). In 1 Corinthians 16:8–9, Paul says: 'I will stay on at Ephesus until Pentecost, because a great door for effective work has opened to me' (NIV) and in 2 Corinthians 2:12, he writes, 'Now when I went to Troas to preach the gospel of Christ, [I] found that the Lord had opened a door for me' (NIV). So, in Revelation 3:8, Jesus is referring to an opportunity for mission. For those who may feel anxious about this, there are two points of additional comfort that Jesus offers.

First, the word used for 'open', *eveogmenen*, is in a tense that suggests a continuous state of affairs: the door is open and will remain open. Too often, young people are anxious about undertaking mission activities in case they 'get it wrong'. They fear that, if they make a mistake or say the wrong thing, it will destroy any further opportunities to share the gospel in that context—but Jesus refutes that fear. He says that the door is open and will remain open. If the young person 'gets it wrong', the door will stay open. If the young person 'says the wrong thing', the door will stay open. If the young person loses their nerve at the last minute and says nothing at all, the door will still stay open. Because of the way the word 'open' is constructed, we can encourage our young people to relax into mission and evangelism. When they are ready, the door will be open.

Second, we note the phrases 'I have given' and 'No one is able to close'. God has ultimate control. He is the Lord of the harvest. Again, this offers a deep sense of release because it means that our young people do not have to shoulder the burden or carry the responsibility for mission and church growth. Their task is to proclaim the gospel of Christ. It is the work of the Holy Spirit to lead others to respond to that message. It is not their responsibility. All we need to do is disciple our young people into the ways of mission and God will grow his church according to his will. He has the keys; we do not. He opens doors and no one can close them. He closes other doors and no one can open them. Jesus Christ is Lord of the harvest.

This is a beautiful way to end our study on Revelation because we conclude by recognising the authority and sovereignty of God. God knows our weakness and vulnerability but he meets us where we are and encourages us. If we remain faithful to him, we are part of the people of God and we will escape the judgment and receive the crown of life. We are assured that we belong to God, that we are citizens of heaven and that an eternity with Jesus Christ awaits us.

As John stood on the shores of Patmos, watching his letter disappear across the horizon in the hands of the messenger, his most earnest desire would have been that those who received it would grow deeper in their love of Jesus and discipleship of God. We have that same desire for the young people we serve today. The concluding words of John's letter, 22:21, form our prayer today: 'The grace of the Lord Jesus be with all.' Amen!

Some questions to consider

- What are your young people most committed to? What does commitment mean to them and how does it manifest itself in their values and behaviour?
- What qualities do your young people look for in a cause to commit to? What are the qualities of the type of leader they would commit to following? How might you creatively present God and Jesus in that way?
- For young believers, what is it about Christianity that inspires them to commitment? For those you know who are not Christians, what is it about Christianity and the church that prevents them from wanting to commit?
- Do you or your church demand too much from your young people in terms of activity and attendance? How might you help them to pace themselves better without risking boredom?
- In what ways do your young people take responsibility for each other? How might you engage them more deeply in mentoring one another in the faith?
- What place does attendance at Christian festivals have for your young people? How do they feel when they return to their home church? How can you make for a positive integration between festival experience and everyday discipleship?
- How can you help your young people to find God creatively in the everyday?
- What does passion for God look like with your young people? How might you seek to encourage those who have become lukewarm in the faith?
- What mission opportunities do your young people have? How might you encourage those who are feeling vulnerable and weak, with little to give when it comes to evangelism?

Some final questions

- In the light of all that you have learned from the book of Revelation, what encouragements have you received in your own walk with God?
- In what areas do you see the need for particular attention so that you might grow stronger in your discipleship and spiritual disciplines?
- What conversations might you need to have to facilitate your own growth with God? Who can you talk to further about this? Who can you ask to support you in prayer as you seek to journey deeper into God?
- Take a moment in prayer. In the light of your study of the book of Revelation, what do you want to say to God? What might he want to say to you?

Bibliography

Aristotle, *The Nicomachean Ethics* (Oxford University Press, 2009)

Arndt, W.F. and Gingrich, F.W., *A Greek-English Lexicon of the New Testament* (Chicago Press, 1979)

Bauckham, R., *The Theology of the Book of Revelation* (Cambridge University Press, 1993)

Barclay, W., *The Revelation of John Vol. 1* (St Andrew's Press, 1974)

Barclay, W., *The Revelation of John Vol 2* (St Andrew's Press, 1976)

Beasley-Murray, G.R., *Revelation* (Eerdmans, 1987)

Brueggemann, W., *Israel's Praise* (Fortress Press, 1988)

Codrington, G. and Grant-Marshall, S., *Mind the Gap* (Penguin, 2005)

Cole, R.A., *Mark* (IVP, 1989)

Collins-Mayo, S. et al, *The Faith of Generation Y* (Church House Publishing, 2010)

Cranfield, C.E.B., *The Gospel According to St Mark* (Cambridge University Press, 1977)

Hendriksen, W., *More Than Conquerors* (Baker, 2007)

Hooker, M., *The Gospel According to St Mark* (A&C Black, 1991)

Lewis, C.S., *The Screwtape Letters* (Geoffrey Bles, 1944)

Morris, L., *Apocalyptic* (Eerdmans, 1972)

Morris, L., *Revelation* (IVP, 1987)

Owen, J., *The Works of John Owen Vol. 3* (Banner of Truth, 1966)

Rowland, C., *The Open Heaven* (SPCK, 1982)

Savage, S. et al, *Making Sense of Generation Y* (Church House Publishing, 2011)

Taylor, C., *A Secular Age* (Harvard University Press, 2007)

Tillich, P., *The Courage to Be* (Yale University Press, 2000)

Wilcock, M., *I Saw Heaven Opened* (IVP, 1975)

Also by Steve Griffiths

God of the Valley

A journey through grief

Beginning with the toughest question—'why?'—Steve Griffiths explores suffering and how we can question, rage, weep and eventually find consolation in God's arms, no matter how desolate our situation. Reflecting on the pain of his wife's long illness and eventual death at the age of 36, he writes as one who has personally known prolonged grief, but also as a church minister who has preached and shared pastorally with bereaved families the insights found in scripture.

ISBN 978 1 84101 826 3   £6.99
Available from your local Christian bookshop or, in case of difficulty, direct from BRF: please visit www.brfonline.org.uk

Pioneers 4 Life

Explorations in theology and wisdom for pioneering leaders

There is a growing awareness that the church must commit to radically new agendas and fresh initiatives in order to connect the gospel with the widest possible spectrum in our society. Faith, commitment, sacrifice and boldness are needed—and an emerging generation of pioneering leaders focused on breaking new ground and growing Christian communities where none has flourished for many years, if ever.

This book emerges from the shared experiences of those attending the Breakout Pioneers Conference, an annual three-day gathering of pioneer church leaders. Established to seek out and draw together pioneers, the gathering also looks to support and train them so that they are free to pioneer as God leads them.

Contributors include:

- Graham Cray
- George Lings
- Lucy Moore
- Mike Moynagh
- John Drane
- Richard Bauckham

ISBN 978 1 84101 827 0   £8.99
Available from your local Christian bookshop or, in case of difficulty, direct from BRF: please visit www.brfonline.org.uk.

Enjoyed

this book?

Write a review–we'd love to hear what you think.
Email: reviews@brf.org.uk

Keep up to date–receive details of our new books as they happen.
Sign up for email news and select your interest groups at:
www.brfonline.org.uk/findoutmore/

Follow us on Twitter @brfonline

By post–to receive new title information by post (UK only), complete
the form below and post to: BRF Mailing Lists, 15 The Chambers, Vineyard,
Abingdon, Oxfordshire, OX14 3FE

Your Details
Name _____
Address_____
_____
Town/City _____ Post Code _____
Email_____

Your Interest Groups (*Please tick as appropriate)	
☐ Advent/Lent	☐ Messy Church
☐ Bible Reading & Study	☐ Pastoral
☐ Children's Books	☐ Prayer & Spirituality
☐ Discipleship	☐ Resources for Children's Church
☐ Leadership	☐ Resources for Schools

Support your local bookshop
Ask about their new title information schemes.